Tales of the Ex-Apes

Tales of the Ex-Apes

How We Think about
Human Evolution

Jonathan Marks

UNIVERSITY OF CALIFORNIA PRESS

University of California Press, one of the most
distinguished university presses in the United States,
enriches lives around the world by advancing scholarship
in the humanities, social sciences, and natural sciences. Its
activities are supported by the UC Press Foundation and
by philanthropic contributions from individuals and
institutions. For more information, visit www.ucpress.edu.

University of California Press
Oakland, California

Library of Congress Cataloging-in-Publication Data

Marks, Jonathan (Jonathan M.), author.
    Tales of the ex-apes : how we think about human
evolution / Jonathan Marks.
        p.   cm.
    Includes bibliographical references and index.
    ISBN 978-0-520-28581-1 (cloth, alk. paper) — ISBN
978-0-520-28582-8 (pbk., alk. paper) — ISBN 978-0-520-
96119-7 (electronic)
    1. Social evolution.   2. Human evolution.   I. Title.
    GN360.M37   2015
    599.93′8—dc23   2015006790

Manufactured in the United States of America

24   23   22   21   20   19   18   17   16   15
10   9   8   7   6   5   4   3   2   1

In keeping with a commitment to support environmen-
tally responsible and sustainable printing practices, UC
Press has printed this book on Natures Natural, a fiber
that contains 30% post-consumer waste and meets the
minimum requirements of ANSI/NISO z39.48-1992 (R 1997)
(*Permanence of Paper*).

For Peta, who made this possible

CONTENTS

PREFACE

This book is not about paleoanthropology. It does not analyze the supraorbital torus of *Homo erectus,* or the feet of *Australopithecus sediba.* This book is about how to make sense of information like that; it's about thinking. Further, it is premised on an uncontroversial point. Humans are universally interested in who they are and where they come from. Sharks, elephants, bats, chimpanzees, and other species are not. Or if they are, it is only in ways that are inaccessible and unfathomable to us, and always will be.

This fact immediately establishes the case for human exceptionalism. We are different from other species in that we do attempt to situate ourselves in a social and historical universe, and thereby make sense of our existence. We are sense-making creatures—that is one of the functions of our most prominent organ, the brain—and we create that sense in many different ways, culturally. The study of how people make sense of who they are and where they came from is kinship, the oldest research program in anthropology, which is predicated on the oldest systematic observation in anthropology, that different cultures make their own sense of who they are related to and descended from, and their sense-making systems somehow work. Our own ideas of relatedness are always in some degree of flux, and are particularly responsive to economy, politics, and technology.[1]

Our own ancestry is important to us, and the authoritative voices about it are of course those of science. Science itself is cultural, a fact-producing mode of thought, but when it produces facts about our ancestry, those facts are heavily value laden, and thus are often different from other classes of scientific facts. Understanding how those human facts differ from, say, cockroach facts, is the first step toward reading the literature on human evolution critically. And the simplest answer is, Little is on the line, and few people care about cockroach facts. (Of course urban apartment dwellers and the manufacturers of insecticides may sometimes care strongly about cockroach facts; but those cares are quite specific and localized.) In addition to being facts of nature, human facts are political and ideological; history shows that clearly. It doesn't mean that human scientific facts are unreal and untrue—just that one needs to scrutinize them differently, because there are more variables to consider.

This is not about theories of evolutionary progress or biological teleology, which see evolution as culminating with our species, and which have been a traditionally popular way to reconcile scientific and theological ideas about human origins. These teleological theories have often been accompanied by a view of nature as a linear hierarchy, a Great Chain of Being—which sounds more erudite in Latin (*scala naturae*) and sexier in French (*échelle des êtres*). Personally I don't think we sit atop anything but the food chain, but I don't see how the point can be established without standing outside of the system itself, which is manifestly impossible. One such proof that I recently read explained to readers that "the history of life told by other organisms might have different priorities. Giraffe scientists would no doubt write of evolutionary progress in terms of lengthening necks, rather than larger brains or toolmaking skill. So much for human superiority."[2] But the validity of this argument against human "superiority" involves invoking a rhetorical universe of superintelligent giraffes who apparently require neither big brains to produce scientific thoughts, nor hands to write them down. In other words, the argument dethroning humans ends up establishing exactly the opposite point—because you have to invent human giraffes in order to dethrone human humans.

Our grasp of who we are and where we came from begins with an appreciation that we are the products of naturalistic evolutionary processes, but we are also not separate from the things we are trying to understand; consequently our project is scientifically reflexive. That is the central point of this book: Our ancestors were apes and we are different from them, and we want to know how that happened. We are bio-cultural ex-apes trying to understand ourselves.

This book, then, is about two reciprocal themes: how to think about anthropology scientifically, and how to think about the science of human origins anthropologically. This will be a presentation of human origins, then, which begins with recent work in science studies, to articulate an evolutionary anthropology that is consistent both with modern biology and with modern anthropology, and is more scientifically normative than evolutionary psychology or creationism. My thesis is that what differentiates biological anthropology (the study of human origins and diversity) from biology (the study of life) is reflexivity, the breakdown of the distinction between subject and object that characterizes modern science. One simply cannot have the same relationship to boron or to the planet Jupiter that one has to the ancestors or neighbors. Our scientific narratives of human origin and diversity are just that—narratives, with properties endowed by the "epistemic virtues" of science, notably, naturalism, rationalism, and empiricism. Nevertheless, since they are narratives specifically about who we are and where we came from, they are simultaneously narratives of kinship and ancestry, which are universally culturally important.

I explored the genetic meanings of evolutionary relatedness and ancestry in *What It Means to Be 98% Chimpanzee* (University of California Press, 2002). My next project involved engaging more broadly with science studies. Given C. P. Snow's famous assertion that science could be understood as an anthropologist understands culture, it stands to reason that our understanding of science could be improved by the introduction of anthropological theory and analyses.[3] Recent trends in the history and sociology of science have involved integrating anthropological knowledge and methods to the extent that the field of science studies, while intellectually diverse, generally has a recognizable anthropological element. I attempted to explore the nature of science, calling specific attention to the scientific ambiguities of biological anthropology, in *Why I Am Not a Scientist* (University of California Press, 2011). The present book focuses specifically on the study of our origins, and situates it as a cultural and scientific narrative, with attendant implications for understanding the nature of the facts it produces.

This book was mostly written in 2013–14 during my year as an inaugural Templeton Fellow at the Notre Dame Institute for Advanced Study, for whose support I am immensely grateful. The NDIAS staff—Brad Gregory, Don Stelluto, Grant Osborn, Carolyn Sherman, Nick Ochoa, and Eric Bugyis—created a stimulating and congenial environment in which to write, and of course the John Templeton Foundation made it possible. I am grateful to the other 2013–14 Fellows of the NDIAS, who allowed me to bounce ideas off of them, and gave me very helpful feedback: Douglas Hedley, Robert Audi, Justin Biddle, Brandon Gallaher, Carl Gillett, Cleo Kearns, Scott Kenworthy, Daniel Malachuk, Gladden Pappen, Scott Shackelford, James VanderKam, Peggy Garvey, Ethan Guagliardo, and Bharat Ranganathan. I am especially indebted to the input of the external visitors to my four NDIAS seminars: Agustín Fuentes, Susan Guise Sheridan, Jim McKenna, Jada Benn Torres, Donna Glowacki, Neil Arner, Matt Ravosa, Phil Sloan, Melinda Gormley, Grant Ramsey, and Candida R. Moss. My undergraduate assistants, Iona Hughan and Sean Gaudio, also provided invaluable help in the preparation of this book.

I wish to pay special thanks to the participants in my Templeton Symposium, "The Invisible Aspects of Human Evolution," who helped refine some of the ideas presented herein: Russ Tuttle, Rachel Caspari, Jill Preutz, Deb Olszewski, Anna Roosevelt, Margaret Wiener, Jason Antrosio, Susan Blum, Ian Kuijt, Chris Ball, Agustín Fuentes, Susan Guise Sheridan, Neil Arner, and Rahul Oka.

I am grateful as well to Joel Baden and Neil Arner for comments on parts of this manuscript. Thanks to Karen Strier for decades of encouragement. For their comments on the full text, I owe such a debt of gratitude that several people are going to get yet another mention: Susan Guise Sheridan and Candida R. Moss; Iona Hughan and Sean Gaudio. I also thank Michael Park, Libby Cowgill, and Ashley Heavilon for very helpful comments. And finally and especially, I thank Peta Katz for her help and support and love, while doing all the hard work.

CHAPTER ONE

Science

THE BEGINNING

What am I? Where do I come from? Where do I fit in? These are questions that humans universally ask, and it wouldn't surprise me to learn that they were asked by *Homo erectus* as well.[1]

The answers to these questions come from the fundamentally human domain of kinship. Of course, all creatures have kinship in a narrow, biological sense: sires, dams, maternal half siblings, and the like. Primates "know" their mothers, and often their mother's elder offspring (half siblings), and even their mother's half siblings (aunts). But that is a narrow sense of the term "kinship." Unlike "kinship" in primatology, "kinship" in humans incorporates paternal relations, residence patterns, reciprocal sets of expectations and obligations, the legal status of marriage, the arbitrary division of the social universe into relatives and non-relatives (when of course we are really *all* related), and the transcendence of individual lives and deaths through the "extrasomatic" quality of the lineage. Relatedness extends beyond the limits of your birth and death. The fact that different peoples make simultaneous sense of cultural and biological information by weaving it into a coherent framework for understanding everyone's natural place in the order of things was one of the earliest discoveries of anthropology, as well as its oldest research program: kinship. Kinship comprises the intellectual and social rules for making sense of your own place in relation to everyone and everything else. In short, kinship is orienting. It defines the slots into which people are born and become social, symbolizing beings.[2]

Yet no system of kinship is entirely natural; that is to say, none encodes the interpersonal relations established by geneticists. Our familiar American system gives the same term to the brother that your mom grew up with, and to the bozo who happened to marry your dad's sister. One "uncle" is a relative "by blood" ; another, by legal convention. Of your eight great-grandparents, only one carries your mitochondrial DNA, and thus represents your "matri-line"—as the modern marketers of mtDNA ancestry tests call it (your mother's mother's mother). Yet in the contemporary United States, only geneticists acknowledge that particular relationship to one of your eight great-grandparents as in any way special.

Decades ago, the earliest anthropologists were astonished at the multiplicity of ways that diverse groups of people thought about relatedness. A child might belong to its mother's family or its father's family or both; some roles of a father might be taken over by an uncle; a child might have several fathers; or might not differentiate between siblings and cousins. Or they might differentiate critically between some cousins and other cousins, or between relatives on either side of the family.

However esoteric or bizarre a kinship system might seem, it nevertheless successfully creates an intellectual framework within which you have a good opportunity to survive, cope, cooperate, and breed. More than that, it tells you who you are: daughter of so-and-so, father of so-and-so, descended from a line of so-and-sos, and related to other so-and-sos in certain ways. It answers the existential dilemma, Why continue? Because of the network of obligations and expectations into which you were born, and which you've maintained over the course of your life. You are a part of the past, of the future, and a part of those around you. That is who you are, that is where you came from, and that is your reason for existing—your ancestors, your descendants, and your kin.

That said, however, there aren't too many cultures that believe that they are descended from monkeys or apes. There's sort of one—if we consider post-Darwinian scientific culture to constitute a single, historical, analytic unit. We are significantly related to other species.

But of course, there are many ways to conceptualize a relationship between yourself and other species, aside from a genealogical one. In Transylvania, people change into bats and wolves all the time,[3] but that's not Darwinism. In Chicago, people have special relationships with Bears and Bulls; in St. Louis with Rams and Cardinals, but that's not Darwinism either. Darwinism is about a particular kind of relationship with the animals— a relationship of lineal descent.

But then, there's lineal descent and there's lineal descent. Descent is an aspect of kinship, and it's very meaningful. Very few aspects of language translate well cross-culturally, but if you want to insult someone pretty much anywhere, calling them a "bastard" will usually serve the purpose. After all, it is a direct attack on their descent, implying illegitimacy, the lack of a proper place in the social universe.

Descent is important; indeed it is the bedrock of our most sacred institutions, notably of hereditary aristocracy. Why is Pharaoh on a throne, and not you? Because he has better ancestors. However distinguished you may consider your progenitors, they weren't as good as Isis and Osiris. And that's why you're not the Pharaoh.

The point is that descent is important, some people have better ancestors than others, and raising questions about ancestry is politically relevant. After all, if you want to argue that your ancestors are as good as Pharaoh's, and challenge his right to be there, then you are not only opposing the religious orthodoxy; you are also preaching political revolution. Why are you a peasant? Because your ancestors were peasants. Why are you a slave? Because your ancestors were slaves.

Descent is political. So is religion. In 1776, Thomas Paine publishes *Common Sense,* with the goal of articulating the arguments in favor of democracy and against monarchy. But for thousands of years monarchies had been blessed by the spiritual forces of the universe. From China to Peru, imperial leaders were also religious leaders. In 800 AD, Charlemagne's empire would not be just another Roman Empire, it would be blessed as the *Holy* Roman Empire. And now, in the late 1700s, kings claim to rule by "divine right." And so, a couple of decades after attacking monarchies in *Common Sense,* Tom Paine attacks the religion justifying those monarchies in *The Age of Reason.* He has to; if someone tells you that God likes monarchy, and you don't, then you are obliged either to challenge his knowledge of God, or to acknowledge thinking un-Godly thoughts yourself.

Flash forward a few decades, to 1853. There is political turmoil in Europe. Monarchical institutions are gradually giving way to democratic ones; an increasingly upwardly mobile bourgeoisie is competing with the ancient hereditary aristocracy. An obscure aristocrat named Arthur de Gobineau—calling himself a count, like Monte Cristo and Dracula—writes a defense of the hereditary aristocracy.[4] Why do we need the nobility? Gobineau answers: because they are responsible for civilization. Gobineau thus unites descent with civilization: that is to say, you are civilized because you are from civilized stock, or uncivilized because you come from uncivilized stock. The ruling classes may often seem like lazy, decadent, effete twits, but actually they are responsible for all ten global civilizations (that Gobineau identified), and are also conveniently physically distinguished as "Aryan." Faced with the challenge of finding "Aryans" all over the world, Gobineau imaginatively obliges, explaining that Aryan blood brings civilization, which then declines as the Aryan blood is mixed with that of the locals.

Civilization is thus (in modern vocabulary) in the genes; and it is for this reason that Gobineau is widely known as the father of scientific racism, an epithet obviously not wielded as a compliment. The important thing is to recognize Gobineau's argument as a cry for social stability. It's not about the past so much as it is about the future: the world cannot function without its Gobineaus. They are necessary for civilization; and to supplant them, or to threaten their privileged position (which, of course, they have earned, as the bringers of civilization), would be to jeopardize civilization itself.[5]

Contemporary social philosophers offered little in the way of explicit alternatives. Actually, the term "civilization" had been in use for barely a century, and generally referred to a state of near modernity that was universally attainable, often via missionary work. Civilization was the act of being or becoming civilized, not an organic attribute like a mole or a blood type.

Gobineau's ideas were understandably not widely noted among mainstream social philosophers. Initially promoted by proslavery polygenists in America, such as Alabama's Josiah Nott (who believed that whites and blacks were created separately from one another by God, and thus were of different flesh, for they shared no common descent at all), Gobineau's (creationist) arguments for geneticizing civilization would be repackaged a few decades later by the (evolutionary) conservationist and eugenicist Madison Grant.

Descent and ideology—political, religious, whatever—are all intertwined as part of that historical, social, superorganic miasma we call "culture." They always have been. The mistake is to think that somehow today we can tweak one aspect of culture without affecting another aspect.

SCIENCE AND GENETICS

Science, however, stands outside of culture, as an objective means of finding truth.

Just kidding.

Of course science doesn't stand outside of culture. It's carried out by people who are cultural actors themselves. It has languages and codes of behavior. It's full of political, economic, ideological, and personal conflicts of interest. It radiates with cultural authority, however, which is why all kinds of people and ideas that have no business being called science or scientific often claim to be so anyway.

If we regard science as a "culture," as C.P. Snow famously suggested some decades ago, then scientists are natives, the ones carrying out the scientific activities. By direct implication it takes anthropology to understand what they are doing. Hence, the "anthropology of science."[6]

The study of how scientific knowledge is produced is one of the most relevant and challenging endeavors of contemporary anthropology. How does science manage to progress, and successfully appeal to value neutrality and objectivity, in spite of the diverse interests of its practitioners? Certainly in the area of biomedicine, financial conflicts of interest are so rife that it is hard to know what claims are credible, even in the peer-reviewed literature.[7] Weapons research is driven by nationalistic political concerns, and much of it is classified information; so how can we look to that as a model of science either?

The scientific study of heredity in particular, however, has the most subtle and insidious conflict of interest, for it lays claim to the voice of scientific authority in matters of descent, that most precious element of symbolic human capital. If we take the discovery of Mendelian genetics in 1900 as the maturation of the field, we can have a look at the very first textbook of Mendelism, called *Mendelism,* and published in 1905 by Reginald C. Punnett, and we will note a very curious punch line. Here is that book's last sentence:

> Permanent progress is a question of breeding rather than of pedagogics; as our knowledge of heredity clears, and the mists of superstition are dispelled, there grows upon us with ever-increasing and relentless force the conviction that the creature is not made but born.[8]

That is not so much a statement of fact as a statement of faith. The study of genetics doesn't tell us that the creature is born, not made. It tells us *how* the creature is made; that is to say, it studies the transmission of biological features. But it certainly doesn't tell us that the biological features are the most important ones, which is obviously a highly self-interested statement for a geneticist to make.

The idea "that the creature is not made but born" is not what the field of genetics is about at all. It's a highly ideological assumption about the human condition, and frankly, if that's what genetics is about, then it is a faith-based initiative, like creationism, and probably shouldn't be taught in schools. Genetics is the study of the intergenerational biological transmission of features. As such, it is no more important than ecology or anatomy or any of a host of other naturalistic disciplines; and its subject matter is not really the guiding beacon of your life.

To understand the political issues at stake here, we have to go back to the origins of large-scale social inequality, which has arisen over the last 10,000 years or so, as humans began settling down and acquiring possessions, which it didn't make much sense to acquire before settling down, since it would just be more stuff to pack up and take when they moved on. With sedentism comes possessions, with possessions comes wealth, and with wealth comes inequality. Which brings us back to the question we asked earlier: How come you're not the Pharaoh?

Or more broadly: Why are there great disparities in wealth? Why are there haves and have-nots? Why is there inequality?

To which there are two broad categories of answers. The first answer is that the fact of inequality is to be explained by historical injustice, that is to say, by human agency—of the greedy and evil sort. In this scenario, then, we work for social justice to ameliorate the disparities of wealth and power that we see and experience.

The second answer is that there is inequality, to be sure, but that inequality is not an expression of injustice, but rather is a manifestation of an underlying disparity of innate qualities. This is a modern version of Arthur de Gobineau's answer. People have what they deserve, and if you don't have much, well, tough. You don't deserve it. In this scenario, by contrast, we work to demonstrate the existence of the natural inequality that we have hypothesized to explain the social inequality we observe. And what better way to demonstrate the existence of an invisible fact of nature than scientifically?

Science is relevant in this second answer to a much greater extent than it is in the first answer, where working for justice was the goal. The second answer almost pleads with science to identify and locate that invisible natural hierarchy that rationalizes the social hierarchy. And it would be impolite—nay, downright rude—for science not to try and oblige.

The trick here is to remember that natural science isn't necessarily important to the idea of building a just society. When segregationists argued in 1962 that black children and white children shouldn't be in the same schools because the black race was 200,000 years less evolved than the white race,[9] not only wasn't the relevant science very competent,[10] but it didn't matter. All citizens are entitled to equal rights, *irrespective of their biology or innate abilities.*[11] (Although it would be nice to get the biology and measurements of innate abilities right, too, obviously.) Ironically, decades later, animal rights activists inverted the fallacy, arguing that chimpanzees might be entitled to human rights *because they are so smart*—as if rights ought indeed to be allocated on the basis of a presumptive measurement of innate intellectual ability.[12]

This asymmetry in the role of science in explaining the origins of social inequality—history or biology—is why one rarely hears of positive claims "proving" the same general intelligence or innate abilities of disparate peoples. That side tends to be reactive against the claims of every generation to have finally "explained" social inequality naturalistically. In one generation it is the size of the head; in another, the shape; or the averaged scores in a standardized test; or the percentage of the "feeble-mindedness allele" in the different gene pools; or the micro-cephalin allele. The Nobel laureate James Watson probably said it best in 2007, as the *Sunday Times* (London) reported:

> He says that he is "inherently gloomy about the prospect of Africa" because "all our social policies are based on the fact that their intel-ligence is the same as ours—whereas all the testing says not really", and I know that this "hot potato" is going to be difficult to address. His hope is that everyone is equal, but he counters that "people who have to deal with black employees find this not true." He says that you should not discriminate on the basis of colour, because "there are many people of colour who are very talented, but don't promote them when they haven't succeeded at the lower level." He writes that "there is no firm reason to anticipate that the intellec-tual capacities of peoples geographically separated in their evolu-tion should prove to have evolved identically. Our wanting to reserve equal powers of reason as some universal heritage of humanity will not be enough to make it so."[13]

The obvious paradox is that the speaker is a molecular geneticist, but he's not talking about molecular genetics. He's just talking about why he thinks the intelligence of Africans isn't the same as "ours." So, as the Brits quickly appreciated, the racist ideas of a Nobel laureate molecular geneticist are no smarter than the rac-ist ideas of a plumber or cab driver. They kept him on the front page of the newspapers for a week, looking increasingly ghoulish, canceled his speaking engagements, and drove him out of the country. A modern society that strives for social justice can't be bothered with the prejudices of foreign scientists.

Any thoughtful person can enumerate all kinds of reasons to think that the general intelligence of large groups of people has evolved to be roughly the same. First, human evolution has been principally the evolution of adaptability, not of adaptation; that is to say, we evolved to be intellectually flexible, not static. Polar bears "evolved" a fur coat; humans "evolved" guns to shoot polar bears and knives to skin them and used their fur coats to keep ourselves warm. And as far we know, pretty much any human can learn those skills. Second, in concert with that understanding of human evolution, immigrant studies show that people can fully adopt any different lifeways in a generation or two. Names change, accents disappear, and economic advancement seems to make everybody look just a bit less alien and threatening. Third, we solve our problems principally technologically these days, and have been doing so for quite a while, and technological change is not a function of intellectual ability, but of social process. Food production didn't begin with a discovery that seeds caused plants, which is known by modern hunter-gatherers; but with the decision to utilize that knowledge in a systematic way. It's not about invention, but about adoption; and that is not a question of genius, but of social action. Fourth, how naive do you have to be to think that you can measure peoples' innate intellectual capabilities independently of their lived experiences? It's hard enough even to conceptualize what the "innate intellectual capacities" supposedly independent of history might even mean. You don't really think that Einstein would have invented calculus, and Newton relativity, if their lives had simply been switched, do you? More to the point, there are simply no facts about modern Africa that can be understood external to the history of slavery and colonialism, and only by recourse to some form of raw, organic brainpower.[14] And fifth, the social upward mobility that has been achieved in the last half century would have been unthinkable a half century previously; the proper scientific conclusion ought to be that we can expect it to continue, not that it has now met an invisible genetic force field.

I was in Edinburgh at the time of James Watson's British tour, and had a ticket to hear Watson give the Enlightenment Lecture (Watson's invitation was rescinded), and it got me to thinking about another asymmetry in science. Watson was making head-lines as a racist scientist—that is to say, as an articulator, even if not necessarily an actual adherent or activist, of now-rejected social and political ideologies. Yet he wasn't booted out of sci-ence for those beliefs; he was merely booted out of England. There is a place in science for racists.[15]

Suppose Watson instead had been a creationist. Then he would probably have remained in England, but gotten booted out of science, for articulating a set of now-rejected social and political ideologies. Creationism is an ideology, after all; it is ori-enting in terms of telling you where you came from and how you fit in, and it is highly political. Its advocates have tried to use the judicial system repeatedly in the last century to give it a leg up on its empirically and theoretically stronger alternatives. And if you are a creationist—that is to say, someone who believes that the human species has a supernatural origin, and is genealogi-cally separated from all other life—then you don't have a future in science.

So one ideology—being a racist—makes you a bit of an embar-rassment to other scientists, but allows you to continue to live and work among them. And another ideology—creationism—is just so incompatible with science that "creationist scientist" is a con-tradiction in terms, an oxymoron in respectable academic circles.

So why isn't "racist scientist" an oxymoron too? Why is it more acceptable to be a racist in science than to be a creationist? The racist believes that because of membership in a particular, ostensibly natural group, some people are inherently less worthy than the members of other, ostensibly natural groups. That view is about as disproved as creationism is, and in equally indirect ways. After all, when a creationist says, "Nobody has ever seen one species change into another," they are right, but not because species don't change. Rather, the timescale makes it impossible for a single person to actually witness it. Consequently, we have to rely on more indirect evidence, which is nevertheless quite compelling to an open-minded skeptic. Like germs, which you can't see, but which apparently can nevertheless still hurt you.

The jury is *not* still out on the issue of whether racial assignment predicts different sets of innate mental capabilities. We—that is to say, anthropologists—looked very hard for a very long time to try and identify such innate racial mental features, and eventually came to realize that it is a fool's errand. More to the point, it is a racist fool's errand. The problems of Africa are social and political, not biological. And anyone who thinks otherwise is being just as anti-scientific as anyone who thinks the universe was zapped into existence 6,000 years ago.

EVOLUTIONISM AND RELATIVISM

The scientific study of our beginnings is founded on two scientific principles: evolution and relativism. Each has multiple meanings, so let us be precise. Evolution here refers to *the naturalistic production of difference,* and its referent is not stars (as in "the evolution of the solar system"), nor human artifacts (as in "the evolution of the airplane"), nor a single body (as in the development or "evolution" of an embryo into an old fart, as the term was most widely used in Darwin's time[16]). It refers here to groups of organisms, that is to say, biological populations—with some of its processes applying to the differentiation among organisms in the same population, and some applying to differentiation among organisms in different populations. The populations may be parts of the same species, in which case we can talk of microevolution; or of different species, in which case we can talk of macroevolution. Moreover, we can examine the fates of particular lineages themselves, and thus talk of the origins of species and the terminations of species (speciation and extinction, respectively).

Relativism here refers *not* to the nihilistic position that there are no rules; that is to say, that because I read somewhere that the traditional Eskimos and Yanomamos beat their wives, therefore I should be allowed to beat my wife. It rather means something close to the opposite: every society, including yours, has standards of behavior, and what you think the Eskimos or Yanomamos do is irrelevant to what you should be doing.[17] Nevertheless codes of behavior, including yours, are historically produced, and are thus understandable not as being transcendent and immutable, but as situated and fallible. We don't stone witches any more, even if the Bible says we should.[18]

Other codes are also the results of history, of human agency, and social process. Consequently in order to make sense of diverse human behaviors, you cannot understand them as crude imperfect approximations to your own behaviors, but only as the products of different histories. As mundane as this may sound today, it is quite directly analogous to other intellectual shifts that took place in the eighteenth century. In one case—biology—Carl Linnaeus, Swedish botanist/physician, argued that species ought not be judged in relation to how similar they are to humans, but by how similar they are to one another. He thus undermined the traditional one-dimensional view, which saw species as comprising a "Great Chain of Being" or "Scale of Nature."[19] By establishing the place of a species only in relation to other species, and not in relation to our own species, Linnaeus was relativizing biological systematics. One kind of metaphorical hierarchy—a ranked, linear hierarchy—was being replaced by another, a hierarchy of inclusion, of various sets within sets. Linnaeus's inference about the pattern of nature would sweep through the academy with only minor opposition, although it would be another century before that nested hierarchy—those sets within sets—would be explained as the trail of common ancestry, by Darwin.

About the same time, of course, there were those preaching that all people (or at least, all white men) should have equal rights as citizens under the law, which went counter to the long-held and well-entrenched view that they shouldn't. Maybe a monarchy headed by a king sitting atop a social ladder, against whom all subjects would be differently gauged according to their status at birth, is a worse situation than a republic, in which all citizens might be entitled to things like liberty, equality, and brotherhood. Once again, a linear hierarchy is replaced by a relativizing framework.

European philosophers had been grappling since the mid-1600s with the question of whether civilization represented progress or decadence. Was "the savage" a near animal, living in a state of perpetual war, or was he somehow deserving of our admiration? After all, the most natural human social relationship was not master/servant, but the free and easy equality of primitive peoples.[20]

World War I pretty much ended that debate, as the most technologically advanced peoples showed themselves to be simultaneously the most barbaric peoples. Death from a lion or cobra in the jungle didn't seem quite as bad any more, when compared to a horrible death from poison gas on the front, or the terror of aerial bombardment.[21] So if civilization could be considered progress only if we considered arbitrary, narrow aspects of it—say, bracketing off technology from all other aspects of civilization—then what good was the concept of progress? There was adaptation—to climate, politics, and economics—but all groups of people adapted, although they did it differently, and in response to different stimuli, like the stimulus of new technologies and social circumstances.

So as long as people were human, they would now be seen as fully cultural beings—not more or less cultural than us, or than anybody—just *differently* cultural. Their cultural similarities and differences were the products of history, and their physical, biological, craniological, or genetic patterns of similarity were correlated variables, but irrelevant to a causal analysis of cultural forms. Just as eighteenth-century biology rendered it decreasingly sensible to measure all animals against *Homo sapiens,* twentieth-century anthropology rendered it decreasingly sensible to measure all cultures against modern urban America. You could compare things, to be sure, but comparisons would be made horizontally, or non-judgmentally, as it were—as one might compare a buffalo to a scorpion. There are enviable and unenviable aspects of each, but they are both good at what they do, which is to survive, adapt, and breed as buffaloes and scorpions.

So too with human cultures, but with one important difference. Since cultures are the products of human thought and activity, a full understanding of them is necessarily experienced, and cannot really be objectified. This horizontal, experiential, comparative understanding of lifeways, already entrenched in American and British anthropology, was popularized in Ruth Benedict's 1934 book, *Patterns of Culture,* as "cultural relativity."[22] (Albert Einstein had won the 1921 Nobel Prize in part for showing that things as apparently invariant as mass and time could be experienced differently at the speed of light—and of course used the same word. Quite possibly the ideas were independently derived from nineteenth-century German philosophy. But I suspect that the early anthropologists were capitalizing on the publicity of the physics.)

Most importantly, then, it was no longer scientific to see different human lifeways as the products of superior or inferior individual intellects. That would be the equivalent of the natural philosophy of the Bridgewater Treatises in the 1830s and 1840s.[23] Erudite perhaps, but premodern. Our species differentiated by naturalistic process from earlier species—and miracle is no longer considered explanatory here; and we also differentiated by historical process from earlier cultural systems, and genetics is no longer considered explanatory here. Indeed, to look for genetic explanations for social-historical facts is like looking for miracles. It's obsolete, ideologically based, unscientific, and should not be countenanced as science. Worse yet, it gives science a bad name (something that creationists, climate change deniers, and UFOlogists are not able to do), by making science into simply another tool for the maintenance of social inequality.

Science is supposed to be liberatory, not oppressive.

Because of the asymmetry of the role of science in the two claims, the rule of thumb has got to be, Any claim to validate human social inequalities scientifically is probably bogus. Every such claim up to this point has been shown to be so. And that is indeed a pretty fair encapsulation of the history of physical anthropology.

PHYSICAL ANTHROPOLOGY

It is hard to look at the history of the study of human origins and diversity and not see it as a transformation from a science of oppression to one of liberation. The field began with the study of the correlated diversity in appearance and behaviors. Exotic peoples not only acted exotic, but they looked exotic as well. Their enslavement or destruction or exploitation at the hands of Europeans had its bleeding-heart critics, to be sure, and an axis certainly existed on the question of whether exotic peoples were irredeemably exotic, or just like us but slightly different.[24] Physical anthropology was the science that made the correlated variables into causal variables: people looked different and acted different, because they really were different, and physical anthropology studied the naturalistic aspects of that difference.

It was everywhere politicized early on. In the United States the "American school" of physical anthropology were apologists for slavery, citing the stability of racial features, and often inferring separate origins for the races on that basis (polygenism). The science was mooted by the Civil War, and not really revived until the recruitment of Aleš Hrdlička by the Smithsonian at the turn of the century.[25]

In England, the question of one or separate origins for the human races divided interested scholars into the (monogenist) "Ethnologicals" and the (polygenist) "Anthropologicals," each with their own society and publications. Charles Darwin and Thomas Huxley were "Ethnologicals," and Huxley was the last president of the Ethnological Society of London. Huxley oversaw the absorption of the rival of the Ethnological Society, which took its rival's name, becoming the Anthropological Institute of Great Britain and Ireland in 1871, and later, the Royal Anthropological Institute.[26]

On the Continent, relations were invariably tense between France and Germany, as Germany became unified and militarized under Otto von Bismarck. In the heat of the Franco-Prussian War, the physical anthropologist Armand de Quatrefages claimed to have demonstrated cranially that Prussians were not even true Europeans at all, but interlopers, related to the Finns. In response, the Germans insisted that "race" and "nation" were not so tightly connected, and began the first systematic anthropometric survey of their population, which began to disentangle the concepts of "race," "nation," and "type."[27] It is an irony of history that the intellectual descendants of those first German anthropologists were the students of Franz Boas in America; while German anthropology itself was eventually hijacked by the naturalizers and synonymizers of race, nation, and type.

So everybody used the science for political ends and denied that they were doing it, for that wouldn't be good. It was always someone else doing it.

Columbia University saw the value in a specialist in the bodies of exotic peoples, and recruited Franz Boas, whose principal research lay in measuring schoolchildren and the indigenous peoples of Canada. A few years later, the Smithsonian hired Aleš Hrdlička, and about a decade later, Harvard hired a classicist/archaeologist named Earnest Hooton. Boas would turn to cultural anthropology, Hrdlička would devote himself to organizing and museum research, and Hooton would become a celebrity academic at Harvard, and train the next generation of physical anthropologists.

Franz Boas and Earnest Hooton had a cautious, but respectful relationship. Boasian anthropology was descended from the first-generation Berlin anthropologists who had begun dissociating the natural from the cultural, and were founding a science of ethnology—the scientific, comparative analysis of human cultures—on the basis of a "psychic unity of mankind."[28] In other words, the wiring of the brain is irrelevant to understanding the basis of human social and cultural differences; it is functionally a constant, and you can't use a constant to explain a variable.

Hrdlička's anthropology, on the other hand, was derived from that of the French craniological school;[29] and Hooton's from the archaeologists at Oxford. Both groups tended to place rather more weight on biological difference as explaining behavioral difference. Hooton, in particular, struggled to differentiate (good) American racial anthropology from (bad) German racial anthropology in the 1930s. But he was unsuccessful, for both were saddled with the same false assumptions about the causal nature of the relationship between biological difference and cultural difference. In 1936, when Boas circulated a petition condemning Nazi race science among the leaders of the physical anthropology, only Hooton and Hrdlička would sign on. Most other physical anthropologists, like Raymond Pearl of Johns Hopkins, respectfully declined.[30]

But Hooton clung to the idea of state-controlled breeding programs well into the 1930s, after most American scientists had begun backing away from it, which was partly in reaction to the enthusiasm with which the Nazis were embracing it. In 1937, Hooton made the *New York Times* with a speech to a group of Harvard alumni in Kansas City, in which he called for the improvement of modern society by encouraging only the fittest to breed, and for a "biological purge upon the unfit." Two years later, he published his magnum opus, *The American Criminal*, Volume I, which statistically analyzed the faces and bodies of criminals and contrasted them against the faces and bodies of volunteer firemen in three different states, purporting to demonstrate a corporeal dimension to criminality. It was so poorly reviewed that Harvard University Press never published a second volume.[31]

After World War II, Hooton's students populated the chairs of physical anthropology in the United States, and transformed the discipline. This transformation was spearheaded by Sherwood Washburn's vision of a "new physical anthropology," which would centralize human evolution, incorporate primate studies, and restructure the study of human physical diversity as the study of how human groups adapt and change bioculturally, rather than as a naturalistic pseudoexplanation for human behavior.[32] The Boasians had got it right after all: the greatest component of human diversity is its cultural component. If you analytically—and perhaps perversely—separated out the minor component of human diversity that is biological, rather than cultural, you would find its major feature to be cosmopolitanism, or the same variations appearing in many groups, rather than differences between the groups. As articulated in the 1951 UNESCO Statement on the Nature of Race and Race Differences, "With respect to most, if not all, measurable characters, the differences among individuals belonging to the same race are greater than the differences that occur between the observed averages for two or more races." Moreover, if you ignored the cultural and the biologically cosmopolitan, what now remained of human diversity was principally clinal—that is to say, distributed in geographical gradients. And what was left without the cultural, the cosmopolitan, and the clinal was principally local variation. As the Oxford physical anthropologist Joseph Weiner put it in 1957, we now saw human populations "as constituting a widespread network of more-or-less interrelated, ecologically adapted and functional entities."[33]

If you were interested in human diversity, race was a biological tail wagging a cultural dog. Race was thus defined out of scientific relevance; that is to say, "racial problems" were not really racial at all, they were social problems. Having thus solved the problem of race, physical anthropology was now free to focus on human evolution, microevolution, and primate behavior. Indeed, it began to acknowledge the relevance of data that were "biological," if not quite "physical"—such as behavior and DNA.

SCIENTIFIC ANTHROPOLOGY

What is it that makes the scientific narrative of human origins better than other narratives? Perhaps "better" isn't quite the right word. What makes evolution, or some version of it, a *scientific* narrative, as opposed to creationism (or some version of it)?

Here's the problem. As soon as you establish some criterion for demarcating a scientific from an unscientific practice, it's quite easy to find a science that lacks that property, but is nevertheless still science. Testing hypotheses—Karl Popper's famous criterion—doesn't account for the Human Genome Project, which was purely inductive—we were sequencing the complete human DNA sequence because we could; we knew it was important, and expected that something interesting would fall out of it. Yet nobody doubted that it was science.

What differentiates science is the scientific mind-set, or the "epistemic virtues" you bring to the work.[34] Modern science can probably be reduced to three such ideas: naturalism, empiricism, and rationalism. Naturalism is the assumption that there is a division between the world of spirit and miracle, and that of matter and law; and that a scholar can effectively bracket off the latter and study it separately. The earliest modern ethnographic fieldwork showed how unusual an idea that is. People don't generally conceptually separate the two realms: the world of magic and caprice interpenetrates that of materiality and predictability.[35] And when you think about it, neither do "we" really separate them fully, except in science. Whether in Las Vegas or Wrigley Field or Wall Street, our hopes, dreams, and prayers intersect with the regularities of matter, motion, randomness, and life all the time. Modern people find ways to accommodate both antibiotics and heavenly invocations for health simultaneously. Our coinage, after all, doesn't say, "In representative government we trust," but rather, "In God we trust"—as if the basic issue were appropriate piety, rather than the politics and struggles that ultimately brought about some measures of democracy and freedom. And every night, a non-trivial percentage of graduate students in the natural sciences goes to sleep hoping (and even praying) for positive experimental results.

The point is that separating the two realms is weird, which is why nobody really attempted it until fairly recently. When they started to do it, in Europe in the early 1600s, they called it by code names, like "the Secret College" and "the New Philosophy." Eventually it came to refer to the most reliable and powerful forms of knowledge, as in Francis Bacon's famous axiom, *scientia potestas est,* generally rendered as "Knowledge is power."[36]

The second assumption science brings is empiricism, that ideas must be matched up to perceived reality, and that the former must be adjusted to be consistent with the latter. Once again there is a lot to be taken for granted culturally here. After all, evidence is important in many kinds of non-scientific activities. If you are a reader of chicken entrails or tea leaves, you still have to consult them for the specific omens, which requires knowledge of how to translate observations into predictions. If you want to convict a witch or a traitor, you still have to base it on something; yet neither divination nor law is science.

The kinds of things that architects, engineers, and stonemasons traditionally built—from boats to temples to aqueducts—are based on the application of accumulated knowledge, often trial and error. The ancient Greeks respected this, and called it *techne,* the knowledge for building and doing. But they distinguished that from an understanding of how the universe is put together, and how the things in the world actually work, and where they come from—the order in things—which was a different kind of knowledge, *episteme.* We often maintain a semblance of this distinction in "applied" versus "pure" science, but that's not quite it, for the Greek *episteme* incorporated how to think about nature, or what we would consider philosophy today.

By the seventeenth century, European scholars distinguished natural history from natural philosophy, the former referring to the collection of facts about the world, and the latter referring to a systematic understanding of how the world works. Newton's *Principia* (1687), a work of natural philosophy, nevertheless had implications for understanding the facts of moving bodies. Consequently, throughout the eighteenth century these bodies of knowledge became gradually realigned, so that facts, their understanding, and whatever application they might have would now begin to be embodied in a single person, a "scientist"—a word coined in the 1830s.[37] Darwin's *Origin of Species* (1859), a work of natural history, closed the circle, with its implications for understanding the forces that had produced the facts of life. The point, once again, is that the value of evidence-based comprehensions of the world is not necessarily self-evident. It requires the convergence of several kinds of specialized knowledge. You don't actually need to know about the condensation cycle to know that you need rain for your crops to grow, or to predict when the rains are likely to come.

Finally, we come to the third scientific assumption, a watchword of eighteenth-century scholarship—rationalism, the application of reason to guide the construction of evidence-based explanations. In practice, this means the downgrading of the explanatory power of the miraculous. Over the century that stretched from the Dutch philosopher Baruch (Benedictus) Spinoza in the 1640s to the Scottish David Hume in the 1740s, miracles took a terrible beating within the scholarly community. It wasn't that science was showing that God didn't exist, but that theologically He was being reconceptualized as a motive force in the universe, rather than as a super-father or mega-king.[38] He made the laws by which the universe runs—and those laws forbid the sun from standing still in the sky for a full day, or a star from leading a caravan from somewhere in Iran to a manger in Bethlehem. It was simply much more likely that there was a mistake somewhere—either in the veracity and accuracy of the story or in the understanding of the original witnesses or in the fidelity of the story's transcription since that time. By the 1790s, the history of language was being treated rationally, despite the biblical story of the Tower of Babel. Concurrently, geologists were studying earth history despite the biblical chronology, and a germ theory of disease was gaining popularity in epidemiology as the belief in spirit possession as a cause of illness was on the wane. By the 1830s, even the life of Jesus was being treated rationally, rather than as a series of miracles.[39] A scientific classic of 1890, James Frazer's *The Golden Bough*, began its analysis of the gospel with the radical assumption that the proper frame of reference for understanding it was in the myths and legends of the ancient Near East.

It is the convergence of these three ideas—naturalism, empiricism, and rationalism—that permits us to define the Human Genome Project into science and creationism out of it. Defining creationism out of science, however, does not solve the problem of creationism, any more than defining ancient alien astronauts out of science can solve that particular problem.

CHAPTER TWO

History and Morality

History is more important, in subtler ways, than biology. In neither case am I referring to an accumulation of facts—historical or biological—but rather to the significance of that domain of thought for human life. I'm referring to questions like "How did I get here?" and "What on earth happened?" and not to questions like "Who won the Franco-Prussian War?"

"How did I get here?" is a question that is answerable biologically or historically, although the biological answer would focus on the syngamy of their egg and sperm pronuclei but omit Mom and Dad's passion that led to it, and would also leave out your life experiences that brought you to this point, aside from the constant mitosis and physiological functions.

"What on earth happened?" is a historical question that can also be answered biologically. The bones at the end of your reptilian jaw migrated to the middle ear to join the stirrup as the hammer and anvil of your mammalian jaw. That's what happened, over the course of a few tens of millions of years.

Yet, as any creationist will gladly tell you, it didn't happen at all. The experts are either mistaken or lying. If the experts are mistaken, that implies a radical relativism of knowledge; there is no longer any such thing as expertise, and everybody's ideas are as true as everybody else's. And if experts are lying, then why are they doing it?—and try not to sound like a paranoiac.

Obviously it's important. How important? In the 1920s, the creationists tried to make evolution illegal; later, they tried the relativist route, as "scientific creationism" in the 1970s and "intelligent design" in the 1990s.[1] Obviously this is important; the right to speak with authority about the history of our species is simultaneously religious and political and scientific. In fact, perhaps the most bizarre aspect of the 2011 Miss USA Pageant was the question put to the contestants—"Should evolution be taught in schools?" Several of them stammered through answers to try and look both pious and open-minded, but none observed that the question was reversed, for it ought to have been "Should creationism be taught in schools?" To the pageant organizers, the norm was that creationism would indeed be taught in schools, and the question was framed about the option for Darwinism.

The history of life is not the only contested political arena; the history of America is one, too. In 1994, as the Smithsonian prepared an exhibit on the atomic bomb, a furious political war broke out.[2] The intent was to get visitors to think about the decision to drop the bombs on Hiroshima and Nagasaki in 1945, the immediate aftermath for the Japanese victims, and the beginning of the Cold War. What would casualty levels have been if the Allies had invaded Japan? Was Nagasaki really necessary? Was Truman trying to intimidate our Soviet allies as well as beat the Axis? To outraged militarists, like Charlton Heston and the American Legion, the decision to drop the bombs was such an obviously good one that any attempt to revisit it was equivalent to treason. They successfully derailed the Smithsonian from its mission of public education to one of nationalism for a time, and most importantly, they got the exhibit canceled.

In March 2010, the Texas Board of Education began to downplay the deist Thomas Jefferson in favor of more acceptably Christian founding fathers.[3] History sure is political.

One of the less well-appreciated aspects of the "science wars" of the 1990s was the battlefield of historiography. Since "who gets to write history" and "how it gets written" are invariably about social power, the history of science as written by scientists tends to be quite different from the history of science as written by historians. The history of science by historians tends to privilege discoveries; the history of science by scientists tends to privilege discoverers. It is certainly understandable that scientists would privilege the discoverers in their histories: they are ancestor figures. They can be constructed as heroes, the academic Achilles and Paul Bunyan; and as role models, because—who knows?—a generation from now, you too may be the historical subject, for your own great discoveries. Indeed, history itself can be rendered as a series of leaps from discoverer to discoverer, a time line of how we got to where we are today, by standing on the shoulders of giants, as the greatest of them all, Isaac Newton, said so long ago.

But time lines are for a junior high schooler. That's chronology, not history.

Glorifying the first at something new is very much a cultural value. At the very least it mystifies "firstness." After all, the first was sometimes the first to make it to the patent office. James Watson and Francis Crick were the first to deduce the structure of DNA, but they knew they were in a race, and were only a few weeks ahead of Linus Pauling; in other words, if Watson and

Crick had never been born, we would still have the structure of DNA. If Charles Darwin had never lived, would someone else have discovered natural selection? Of course; we know that because someone else did. Several people, in fact—Alfred Russel Wallace and Herbert Spencer, to name just a couple.[4]

What this suggests is that the discoverer may be less significant than the discovery, and consequently that the first to do/think/build it may be a misplaced emphasis. If several people did/thought/built it independently and simultaneously, that suggests that the conditions under which they did, thought, and built things may have been more important than who they were. Why tell me about the monk Gregor Mendel, whose work on plant hybridization wasn't taken seriously until thirty-five years later (by which time, the same things he discovered had been discovered again)? The historical importance lies with the intellectual separation of intergenerational transmission (genetics) from development (ontogeny) in the late 1800s, which rendered Mendel's work newly meaningful. If Mendel had never lived, we would still know what we do about transmission genetics. So why bother telling me about him? Rather, tell me what it meant to intertwine genetics and development in the 1860s, and what it means to separate them—the intellectual achievement that made Mendel's work from 1865 newly recognizable in 1900.[5]

In other words, the history of science is a history of ideas, things, and relationships. The history of discoverers is just a long-running soap opera.

As a history of ideas, the history of science has its political aspects as well. What to include? Who to include? With or without warts? Does physicist Isaac Newton's asexuality or geneticist Calvin Bridges's hypersexuality or anthropologist Ruth Benedict's bisexuality tell us anything important?[6] Are we writing a peculiarly Freudian history of science? Moreover, there are commonly overt political interests in patronage. Patrons need to be buttered up, as even Galileo recognized at the dawn of science. And one way to accomplish that is to use history to glorify the patron, or to demonize the patron's enemies.

Andrew Dickson White, a distinguished historian and educator, wrote a very erudite and influential two-volume work over a hundred years ago called *A History of the Warfare of Science with Theology in Christendom*. On the face of it, there would seem to be a gross self-contradiction in the title alone, given that most science has been done not in opposition to theology, but in a theological context. After all, Galileo may have been put under house arrest by the Inquisition, but he considered himself a Catholic. In fact, he was friends with the pope—which is why he felt as though he could make fun of the pope in his *Dialogues Concerning the Two Chief World Systems,* which is actually what got him into trouble. Isaac Newton may have had his doubts about the Trinity, but he wrote more about theology than about physics; he just didn't publish it. Gregor Mendel was as much a theological insider as anybody could be.

White's book, however, was a very influential polemic—the history of science as seen through the tunnel vision of the struggles that modern science (circa 1900) was having with Christian theology. Science represents reality, the future, wisdom, technology (all of which are actually often poorly correlated variables); religion represents backward tradition, false authority, and ignorance—and what's more, it has always been that way!

It was an erudite and interesting approach to the history of science, but hardly fair and balanced.

Seeing history through the lens of modern issues and concerns is hard to avoid, but it is properly regarded as merely a predecessor to modern scholarship. That is to say, we now understand the past through the issues of the past, not through the issues of the present. The particular issues of today are irrelevant to what the people long ago were doing and thinking (because those issues didn't exist yet), and would be to a large extent untranslatable to people of another age.

And yet there might be some common themes that stretch through times, and across places. The eighteenth-century French naturalist Count de Buffon was indeed forced by the theology faculty of the Sorbonne to recant, in the 1753 fourth volume of his *Natural History*, several things he had said in the first three volumes in 1749. He published ten paragraphs of such backpedaling, but went on to publish thirty-one more volumes, with varying degrees of impiety. But one bit of his 1753 apology was quoted by the influential English geologist Charles Lyell over seventy years later:

> I declare that I had no intention to contradict the text of Scripture; that I believe most firmly all therein related about the creation, both as to order of time and matter of fact; and I abandon everything in my book respecting the formation of the earth, and generally all which may be contrary to the narration of Moses.[7]

And of course, Darwin devoured Lyell's book while in the Galapagos. So isn't it fair to draw a line connecting Buffon, Lyell, and Darwin? And *The State of Tennessee v. John Thomas Scopes* (1925) and intelligent design (2010)?

Well, yes, but only if you can justify why the concerns of eighteenth-century Catholics, nineteenth-century Anglicans, and twentieth-century Baptists would necessarily be identical. And of course, the age of the earth (Buffon and Lyell's primary issue) is not the same as the transformation and genealogy of species (which neither Buffon nor Lyell in the 1830s believed). So, might the issue be not necessarily religion per se, but rather social authority? After all, how do scientists react when their authority is challenged?[8] How do policemen react? How do nightclub bouncers react?

Obviously nobody likes to have their authority challenged, and they will exercise the social power at their disposal to try and prevent it. To frame the conflicts as religion versus science is to miss what really binds the historical episodes. Further, to frame them as regressive religion versus progressive science is to miss a significant chunk of history—the times when science was actually wrong.

When is science wrong? To follow Popper's famous falsification criterion, that science proceeds by proving things wrong, the answer would have to be "usually." So that's not a very good argument against religion. Copernicus was right in placing the earth at the center of the solar system, but wrong about the sun being at the center of the universe, the paths of planets being perfect circles, and the stars being equidistant and attached to a solid sphere. Galileo was impiously right when he said in the early 1600s that the earth goes around the sun, but Charles Bonnet was piously incredibly wrong when he said in the late 1700s that women contain their babies miniaturized in their own ovaries, and those babies contain their own miniature babies in their ovaries, until the final generation. That is not to say that Galileo should not have been persecuted for his radical ideas, and Bonnet should have been, but rather that the significant issue concerns institutions with the authority and power to persecute, not rightness and wrongness as judged in hindsight.

Hindsight, after all, is an optical illusion. Even in ancient times they knew that histories differed according to the viewpoint and interests of the writer. To the victors, a wartime triumph tends to seem inevitable, the result of superior forces, superior cunning, or superior natures. To the vanquished, it tends to seem more precarious, a bit of an unlucky break somewhere turning the tide against them.

The history of science, as written by scientists, is the history of the victors. It is the time line of inventors and discoverers, selected because they were right, or at least because they said something meaningfully similar to what we say today. With the same condescension that accompanies the label "ethnocentric," the time-line approach to history is regarded as "presentist," or somewhat more obscurely, "Whig history."[9] The point is that, in parallel to the ethnocentrists, who can understand another culture only as an imperfect replica of their own, the presentists aren't trying to explain or understand the past—they are simply exploiting the past to the advantage of their modern rhetorical interests.

In this sense, the time-line approach is looking backward from the present, and picking ancestral precursors for their discoveries; but that is *a* history of science, not *the* history of science. After all, what were the other alternatives for each nodal precursor, and what was at stake? Were they the only ones working on the problem? If so, then why wasn't the problem considered more interesting? If not, then what makes this figure the ancestor? How did they manage to discover what had eluded others, and then convince the others of it? Raw brainpower? Gift of gab? A faculty position in the Ivy League? A big grant? And why are so few of the people we talk about women or non-Europeans? Are they just not smart enough to be intellectual heroes, or is our scientific history biased in various ways that we should confront?

Genius is no better an explanation for the history of science than it is for the more general processes of cultural change, as we saw in the previous chapter. In science, everybody is smart; that's why there is so much new discovery. Sure, there are the Stephen Hawkings and the Richard Feynmans, but without them we would still know all the math and physics they would have produced, except a bit later, and from someone else.

In other words, the history of science is about the social production of knowledge, not the neuronal production of knowledge.

A DEPERSONALIZED HISTORY OF EVOLUTION

Armed with the tools of naturalism, empiricism, and rationalism, European scholars of the seventeenth century began to look for, and to find, mathematical regularity—that is to say, order—in the natural world, particularly in the realms of physics and astronomy. The knowledge that the earth could best be understood as a planet orbiting a star suggested that the history of the solar system would naturally somehow incorporate the history of the earth, and moreover, that the history of the earth would somehow incorporate the history of life upon it.[10]

Darwinism—that all species come into existence from previously existing species, and become adapted to their local surroundings by the process of natural selection—is actually a relatively trivial proposition, in the great scheme of things. That is why it is important to see Darwinism as one of several naturalizing scientific discourses of the nineteenth century, the combination of which was so threatening; not as the product of a heroic genius.

The history of evolution, then, doesn't begin with Charles Darwin or his grandfather Erasmus or Jean-Baptiste Lamarck. It begins, rather, with the gradual recognition that life on earth is intimately connected to the history of the world itself, and thus needs to be understood historically. But it also requires fundamentally rethinking the previously heretical idea that knowledge, especially non-biblical knowledge, is good. The compromise effected (principally in England) by theorizing geology and biology, while simultaneously maintaining that this was not a threat to the established social and moral order, came to be known as natural theology. Here, following the lead of the early astrophysicists, the biological realm was seen to be characterized by order, not by chaos. That order was the imprint of God upon the world, and to study it was to testify to God's power and handiwork—in essence, an act of ultimate piety.[11]

The attributes of that order became exposed throughout the eighteenth century. First, extinction (the end of species) was a real phenomenon, with a theologically troubling prospect that God's creations were impermanent. While a naturalist in 1720 could prophesy that a dodo might turn up somewhere other than the island of Mauritius, which is where all the other dodos were from (although one hadn't been seen there since the 1680s), by 1820 the vast reality of extinction (as shown by paleontology) was accepted as a fact of life that required an explanation. Second, the history of life was a succession of life, with the skeletal remains of different kinds of animals superimposed upon one another, tightly fitting with characteristics of the geological features in which they were embedded. And once you have theorized the durations and ends of species, it simply makes sense to theorize their beginnings. Third, living species could be naturally arranged in clusters of increasingly exclusive similarity to one another—for example, identifying monkeys as being simultaneously animals, mammals, and primates. Physically, humans would have to occupy an adjacent spot, as Linnaeus noted in the mid-eighteenth century. What having that spot meant, however, was not immediately clear. And finally, extinct animals, known only from their skeletal remains, might often fall into the known categories but be found in the wrong places (such as elephants in the Arctic), or might crosscut the known categories (such as giant flying or swimming reptiles, like pterosaurs and ichthyosaurs).

The antiquity of the earth was settled by about 1835, with the dismissal of biblical chronology and the confrontation with "deep time."[12] (For contemporary debates, this of course means that a "young earth" creationist has issues not with the science of *The Origin of Species,* but with the science of a few decades before that work.) But as the age of the earth and the history of life became extended backward, human history did not get concomitantly extended. You did not find human remains in geologic strata with plesiosaurs, but only very late in the game, in Roman burials and in ancient tombs, and then looking pretty much like us. It was as if the earth and life upon it did have a history, but the human species did not, aside from its cultural history.

A pious and simple reconciliation of the data would hold that the earth and its inhabitants had a long, unclear prehistory, and that history began with God's placement of Adam and Eve in a (modern) Garden of Eden. This, however, exposed a more interesting question: If Adam and Eve were, say, European-looking, then where did African-looking people come from? Did they come (impiously) from a separate, disconnected origin—which might imply a negative response to the famous question, "Am I not a Man and a Brother?" Or did they come (piously) from the loins of the biblical couple, implying a primordial universal brotherhood, but also the possibility of significant physical change somehow taking place in the human form over a fairly short period of geological time?[13]

Stone tools, which implied the existence of very early people, were increasingly being found in clear association with the remains of extinct animals.[14] This in turn suggested that the disconnect between the premodern world and the Adamic modern world might not be so clear. Philology, tracking the descent of languages from hypothetical reconstructed common ancestors, gained credibility in the early nineteenth century. By about 1820, one major common precursor tongue was widely known as "Indo-European" and was considered to be ancestral to the languages spoken from Ireland to India. Languages clearly had processes of descent and a remote common ancestry in seeming contradiction to the biblical narrative, according to which linguistic diversity simply began ahistorically in Babel. Perhaps it was history all the way down.[15]

As human history and biological prehistory became harder to separate from one another, the question of ancestry and descent naturally came into sharper focus. What, then, was the role of ancestry in creating a human being? Where scholars had previously spoken of "hereditary" factors or diseases, they now began to theorize something called "heredity," consisting of the regularities of transmission. They needed to distinguish the heredity of things like heirlooms from the heredity of things like faces. Moreover, they came to appreciate that the regrowth of a starfish's arm (regeneration), the slight alterations of form needed to derive a civet, a lion, a house cat, an ocelot, and a snow leopard from some hypothetical primordial type of cat-animal (degeneration), and the general processes of reproduction (generation) might all somehow be linked phenomena—especially if you looked at animals in a new way, as clusters of cells.[16]

And the miraculous origin of cells was under assault in biomedicine. Cells were accepted as the "building blocks of life" by
the 1840s, and by 1860 it was very clear that there was only one
way to get cells—from preexisting cells. If we know that cells
don't arise miraculously, and that species are also units of life
but they end naturally, it simply isn't that great a stretch to
maintain as well that species begin naturally, from other species. And many kinds of illness were appearing to be cellular,
from infections to cancers.

There was a transient middle ground between the naturalistic production of cells and species on the one hand, and the
miraculous primordial biblical production of cells and species[17]—namely, the spontaneous coalescence of new cells and
new species under the right circumstances. Nobody could spec-
ify those circumstances, but it had to have happened at least
once, and perhaps cells continued to coalesce spontaneously on
a fairly regular basis. That might imply that the boundary
between the living and non-living is porous, and that life isn't
really that special, much less miraculous. In parallel, given the
succession of species in the paleontological record, it was clear
that species became extinct and were replaced by other species.
Those new species had to come from somewhere. Perhaps new
cells and species occasionally just coalesced into existence,
either miraculously or not.

Okay, not. But it was worth a try.

Yet even for the pious who weren't interested in cells, species,
or languages, the nineteenth century saw the intensification of
biblical scholarship—notably, the attempt to determine what in
the Gospels can be reasonably considered as historical, and what
is likely to be mythological—that is to say, meaningful without
necessarily being accurate. By about 1840, the life of Jesus was

being tackled from the perspective of naturalism, as the German biblical scholar David Friedrich Strauss introduced a field of "higher criticism" of the Bible with his suggestion that the life of Jesus might be productively examined historically. *The Golden Bough*, published in 1890 by the Cambridge classicist and early social anthropologist James Frazer, contextualized the understanding of Jesus in the domain of mythology.

By the turn of the twentieth century, reason and nature had invaded even the most basic elements of Christianity.[18] A backlash soon arose. Darwin was the primary target of the backlash, but there were other aspects of the modern age that soon came under assault as well—notably, liquor. But the backlash against Darwin came from somewhere. In particular, it came from the political conclusions that were being drawn in Darwin's name. The leading expositor of Darwin in Germany was Ernst Haeckel, whose version of evolution traced the struggle for existence from amoebas to the Nordic militarist state. German officers in World War I knew their Haeckel and articulated their aggressive national ambitions in fiercely Darwinian terms.[19] And William Jennings Bryan, a Christian and pacifist, paid attention to them, which helped frame his vision of Darwinism as a fundamentally evil doctrine, and eventually led to his public repudiation of evolution in the *New York Times* in early 1922 on the dual grounds that Darwinism was "harmful as well as groundless."[20]

That raises the interesting question, Suppose the theory of evolution were grounded, but still harmful? That is to say, suppose we came from apes, and therefore ... non-Europeans are lower forms of life? Or therefore ... we should engage in perpetual war until only the fittest survive? Or therefore ... we should sterilize the poor, and restrict the immigration of inferior stocks? Or therefore ... there are no truly selfless acts, and all human behavior must be understood in terms of its self-benefit? Or therefore ... zoos should be closed, and all captive apes should be released into the wild?[21]

All of these have in fact been invoked in the name of evolutionary theory in the last century and a half. But not only are they not actually consequences of Darwinism, but they are also political/moral statements that need to be judged in the political/moral realm, independently of the fact that biological species stand in a historical relationship to one another, produced by the long-term effects of natural selection.

Suppose, for example, that you are a thoughtful citizen who is more concerned with the issue of social justice than with whether we came from monkeys. Then, depending on what version of evolution you were exposed to—and one can hardly expect you to be a highly critical reader, which is the job the scientific community itself is responsible for—you might see the racism, social Darwinism, eugenics, and other things apparently derived from Darwinism as appallingly closed-minded nonsense, *regardless of our relationship to monkeys*. And you might be excused for rejecting the whole kit and caboodle on that basis.

CHARLES DARWIN, ICON

It may seem a distant memory now, but 2009 was a banner year for evolutionary biology—the 200th birthday of Charles Darwin, and (since he was clever enough to publish it when he was fifty) the 150th anniversary of *The Origin of Species*. International symposia extolled his greatness and the correctness of evolution—both of which are valid and accurate. Darwin was indeed a great figure in the history of ideas, and evolution is true.

After a little bit of it, though, historians began to get restless. Could we please move on?

After all, a bit of counterfactual history—if Darwin had never lived—we would still know everything we do. Possibly we would emphasize different things in our comprehension of the history of life,[22] but life would still be understood historically and naturally, not miraculously. Under the premises of naturalism, empiricism, and rationalism, the scholarly community eventually has to hit on the history of life. Further, as George Bernard Shaw pointed out over a century ago, as literature *The Origin of Species* is quite boring.[23] Moreover, a goodly chunk of what gets said in Darwin's name is rubbish anyway. So this must be about more than simply Charles Darwin and *The Origin of Species*.

Of course it is. It's about creationism, and about adopting a figurehead, a heroic ancestor, to lead us into the modern intellectual age. The problem is that by glorifying Darwin and his greatness, we give the creationists an unreasonable idea of his place. But it's not Darwin or *The Origin of Species* that they have issues with; it's the entire field of naturalized knowledge—paleontology, genetics, bacteriology, and the like. We fall into a trap by extolling Darwin: we let creationism drive the scientific agenda.

Why are there creationists? Creationism is a reflection of a basic pedagogical failure on the part of science over the last century and a half: we have failed to convince a lot of people that they are descended from monkeys, and they are very threatened by us and vice versa.

Scientists have occasionally been known to say (correctly) that scientists decide what scientific truth is. More commonly, however, they fail to take the next step, and ask the opposing questions, "What does that actually mean?" and "How would a creationist hear it?" What it means is that, under the agreed-upon conventions for establishing truth in the natural realm, scientists can lay claim to authority in deciding what is likely to be true. Obviously, though, if all parties do not agree initially on the conventions for establishing truth, then science has no claim to authority. Moreover, since science deals with likelihoods and boundary conditions, and much of its day-to-day work involves falsifying ideas from earlier days, science is commonly wrong. What we mean when we say that scientists decide scientific truths is that we want you to believe us in spite of all that, because it is the best shot we have at ever being right. And what *they* hear when we say that scientists decide scientific truths is the arbitrary exercise of intellectual tyranny. We cannot convince the creationists of anything if we disagree fundamentally on how reliable scientific knowledge is produced.

For creationism, then, the battleground has to be epistemological, ideological, and theological. First, how do we come to know something in the modern world? Why are experiments considered more reliable than voices coming out of burning bushes? Second, if the pattern of similarities among living and extinct life-forms does not indicate their general degree of common ancestry, then what does it indicate, especially theologically? Did the almighty Creator get tired and decide to self-plagiarize from body plans He had already used? And third, what are the attributes of a God who takes shortcuts in the creative process, or who makes it look as if the world is ancient and life evolves, if it really doesn't? Ought such a Being to command our veneration?

In other words, creationism is not a scientific issue; it is a cultural issue.

Worse yet, by treating it as if it *were* a scientific issue, we—the human evolution community—have sometimes allowed the creationists to dictate the agenda, and have said things to win their hearts and minds that are untrue, do not stand up well, and simply embarrass the good name of Charles Darwin.

The very first Darwinian generation faced off against the traditionalists, and immediately incurred a debt that subsequent generations of scientists have been paying off. Confronted with the task of trying to convince European readers that they were genealogically connected to apes, in the absence of a fossil record documenting that transition, the earliest Darwinians—most notably Ernst Haeckel—advanced an ingenious argument. The evidence of connection to the apes would come only partially from paleontologists of the future; for the present, that connection was established by the non-European races. Haeckel illustrated the point with a series of grotesque facial caricatures.

In other words, Haeckel was a might quick to sacrifice the full humanity of the non-white peoples of the world, in order to score rhetorical points against the creationists.[24] That is the lesson to query.

The problem here was effectively the desperation of scientists to convince the creationists of their own fundamental truths, thus permitting the creationists to lead the direction of the science. Haeckel marshaled the evidence in support of general evolution, as the leading Continental spokesman for Darwin, but what he had to say about people makes us cringe today. Some contemporary scholars were indeed put off by Haeckel's creative dehumanization of the races of the world, but the fact remained that, to them, he was an ally in the real struggle.[25] Other scholars, who identified the "real struggle" somewhat differently—as a struggle for social justice, not for monkeys as ancestors—found Haeckel's theory of evolution so distasteful that they denounced evolution itself, not having been given adequate tools to distinguish Haeckel's Darwinism from Darwin's Darwinism.

Darwin's Darwinism was first and foremost a theory of kinship. Indeed, the biblical descent of all people from Adam (monogenism; see above) inspired the earliest theories of evolution, since the monogenists had to account somehow for the descent of other human races from whatever race Adam was.[26] Some were attracted to its rival, polygenism, because that seemed to offer a scientific rationalization for slavery—whites and blacks having been created separately, and thereby of different stocks. Others were attracted to polygenism for its consistency with modern science (that of 1840), showing an earth and a history of life to be far older than the Bible suggested; perhaps blacks were created long before Adam and the whites. And still others found polygenism attractive precisely for its theological radicalism, recognizing that the Bible is merely the accumulated lore of the bucolic yokels who inhabited the Near East some few millennia ago.

Darwinism, then, made the science morally respectable—given the arguments about rights and freedom and equality lurking in the background—by giving all people a remote common ancestor, although not Adam. Rather, a kind of ape. Yet within a generation it had been largely superseded by the more chauvinistic, indeed militaristic, variants espoused by the likes of Haeckel and other "social Darwinists"—like paleontologist William J. Sollas, political scientist William Graham Sumner, and sociologist Georges Vacher de Lapouge.[27] A generation later, they were in turn supplanted by the eugenicists, who aimed to build a better society by controlling the microevolution of the American "germ-plasm," which in practice involved working to sterilize the poor involuntarily, and to restrict the immigration of Italians and Jews. Far from being a fringe movement or a pseudoscience, eugenics spoke for much of mainstream biology and genetics; the first significant criticisms of eugenics from within the genetics community came from Raymond Pearl in 1927 and Hermann Muller in 1932, after the Supreme Court had legalized involuntary sterilization of the poor, and Congress had passed legislation to restrict immigration of Italians and Jews—following the recommendations of the biologists.[28]

Decades later, the civil rights movement saw considerable discussion over the role that evolutionary biology had to play in the public debate. There were indeed scientists willing to argue that blacks had evolved to be less intelligent than whites and therefore less deserving of full equality.[29] Others argued that biology is simply irrelevant to a discussion of social justice. By the 1970s it was common to try to make evolution as amoral and as anodyne as possible. Biological anthropology books routinely sidestepped the interesting topic of race in favor of the less interesting topic of population genetics. Likewise, the role of cultural diversity in human life—motivating human life ideologically and arming it technologically, for example—was obscured by debating whether chimpanzees "had" culture.

But then came sociobiology, and evolution became meaningful again. Unfortunately, the meaning wasn't exactly benign again.[30] This time the message wasn't about the semihumanity of non-whites or the need to sterilize the poor on account of their unfitness. Now it was that goodness itself is an illusion, for altruism toward others is either "really" just selfishness toward one's genes (if the altruism is directed at a family member) or toward oneself in the expectation of reciprocation (if the altruism is directed at a non-family member).

At least, that's what studies of insects seemed to show, to some people. To others it suggested that apparent altruism might be the result of the selfish behavior of ideas or "memes" replicating themselves through human action. Anything *except* the possibility that people might actually be nice to one another because it's the right thing to do, and that there are sets of obligations and expectations that anyone learns (that is to say, *evolved* to learn) as a functioning member of a human society, *any* society. In this case the "evolution" of altruism in humans, for the benefit and survival of the group as a superorganism, might simply not result from the same process as the "evolution" of altruism in other animals.

So from the beginning, Darwinism was never simply a transcription of the facts of nature, but was a moral discourse as well. And yet its associated morality has rarely been its outstanding admirable quality. The reason that evolution is a moral discourse is that it is about kinship, and kinship is cultural, and cultural things have a moral dimension. And the lesson of history is this: making evolution morally unacceptable creates an argument for creationism that it would not otherwise have.

OPERATING IN A MORAL UNIVERSE

In any human society, there are things you are supposed to do, things you are allowed to do, and things that you shouldn't do. Knowing the differences among them is maturity. Children can make mistakes and not be held fully accountable, but adults need to know good from evil, and choose good, or else risk the social consequences. Of course, local mores and taboos, and ideas about politeness and respect and morality, vary from place to place, but there is a universal constant: in order to be a member of society, you must follow certain rules. If you don't follow them, we don't want you around.

That might afford a very broadly applicable reading of the Adam and Eve story, whose climax involves the protagonists realizing two facts that they had never cared about before—that they are naked in public, and that it is wrong to be so.[31] This is the transformation from an immature and naive state to the grown-up status of knowing the difference between right and wrong. Once you know it, there is no turning back. You have three choices: never learn it, learn it and disobey, or learn it and obey. The first choice, amorality, is the mythic state you can dream about but never return to, when you could do anything and not be held accountable for it; but now it is restricted to children, animals, foreigners, and primitive ancestors, all of whom can be at least partially excused for not knowing the rules. The second choice, immorality, leads to punishment, stigma, and exile—the mark of Cain. And the last choice, morality, is the obvious expectation, normal human existence with the burden of rules and obligations. In other words, the amoral life (where good and bad don't exist), the immoral life (Cain murdering his brother and lying about it), and the moral life experienced by growing up in a human society (after eating the fruit of the Tree of the Knowledge of Good and Evil—Genesis 3:5—although after a medieval gloss, we call it an apple), comprise the universe of options—and amorality is no longer available. Be moral or immoral, and be prepared for the consequences if you choose the latter.

Of course it is an origin myth, but it is only trivially an origin myth about biology. After all, nobody seriously thought that they came from monkeys until the nineteenth century, and since then, the people who have cared about it the most have been scientists. The Adam and Eve story actually serves a much more fundamental purpose as an origin myth, explaining why you should be good, and what it takes to be one of us, which is the most basic element of human society—knowing what our rules are, and following them.

Sometimes you have to do the right thing even if it gets you into personal trouble, as Prometheus learned after bringing us the gift of fire, for which Zeus had his liver pecked out by an eagle on a daily basis.[32]

So social behavior is fundamental to human existence, and it is organized by a code of moral conduct, which is local and variable, but is crucial to defining who we are, and most especially, who *you* are.

No, we do not eat insects and cats, even though they are edible. They're yucky. No, we do not have sex with someone who does not want to have sex with us. That's yucky, too. And we do not have sex with our sister, even if they *do* want to have sex with us. That's incredibly yucky. And to the incestuous bug-eater, we explain that that's just not the way we do things around here, and you had better shape up if you want to hang out with us.

Back to science: the maturation of modern science involves transforming science from an amoral child into a moral adult. It proceeded over the course of the twentieth century, and is still accelerating. The year 1945 saw two revelations for science. First, the complicity of American physicists in building weapons of mass destruction, which were used as they were intended, to kill and destroy, but for a good cause. As the Manhattan Project's leader, J. Robert Oppenheimer, said a few years later, "Physicists have known sin." And second, the complicity of the biomedical community in judging large groups of people to be innately inferior, and discriminating against them, sterilizing them, or even killing them on that basis. We know what the Germans did in the 1930s and 1940s, but we've never really come to grips with the fact that they were inspired by their American counterparts in the 1920s.[33] Nevertheless the infamous 1927 Supreme Court decision of *Buck v. Bell*, which gave states the right to sterilize citizens against their will, was based on the latest American scientific knowledge and expert testimony.[34] By 1936 the Germans were acknowledging their debt to American geneticists, by awarding one of the most prominent activist geneticists, Harry Laughlin, an honorary doctorate.[35] It even came up at the Nuremberg trials, in defense of the Reich commissioner for sanitation and health, Karl Brandt. It didn't help; he was hanged anyway. Geneticists have known sin as well.

Prior to 1945, one could argue, however naively, that science stood aloof from cultural matters like politics and morality. After all, science and warfare have always had connections, long before the Manhattan Project. During World War I, for example, the German chemist Fritz Haber helped the Axis cause by developing chemical weapons, notably poison gas; in opposition to enlisting science in the cause of mass death were Haber's wife, Clara, and his friend Albert Einstein. Clara soon committed suicide over it; Einstein eventually signed the letter to Franklin Roosevelt that got the Manhattan Project started.

The theme of the scientist without morality has been a literary apprehension since the dawn of science. Francis Bacon's contemporary Christopher Marlowe wrote of a scholar named Doctor Faustus, who seeks the knowledge and power that science touts, but who shortcuts the methods of experiment and observation by simply selling his soul to Mephistopheles. Two centuries later, Mary Shelley wrote of Victor Frankenstein, who acquires the knowledge to reanimate life, but not the wisdom to use it well. And almost two centuries after that, Michael

Crichton wrote of John Hammond, whose desire is to profit from dinosaurs, whose shortcut to knowledge is his checkbook, and who can simply enlist the science and the scientists he wants by buying them. What these characters share is the author's suspicion that "pure knowledge" isn't really the scientist's sole motivation. Doctor Faustus wants sex (with Helen of Troy), Dr. Frankenstein wants life, and Mr. Hammond and his scientific staff want money—the same three base motivations that inspire everyone else, except that these guys are smarter and more ambitious than the rest of us, and actually seek the power that Francis Bacon was talking about when he said, "Scientia potestas est."

So by the second half of the twentieth century a scientist could no longer invoke the separation of science from society. The amoral universe of the primordial Garden is now the moral/immoral universe of infecting Guatemalan prostitutes with syphilis to track its spread,[36] harvesting the cells of Henrietta Lacks and not sharing the wealth they generated with her descendants,[37] proposing imaginary natural inequality as a rationalization for real economic and social inequalities,[38] starting direct-to-consumer genetic services that may market information and misinformation about descent, race, health, or athletic potential, with hardly any oversight or regulation,[39] and producing and vending genetically modified foods and psychiatric pharmaceuticals whose actual value to the human race is less clear than their profitability for their multinational corporate manufacturers.

The issue of interest-conflict is of course an old one. Compromising with the truth in order to maximize profit is, after all, the lifeblood of capitalism. It's salesmanship, showmanship, and marketing, the sucker born every minute, and the proverbial root of all evil. You want to mix that with science? What could possibly go wrong with that?

Actually the intersection of science and profits presents such an obvious conflict of interests that we can even find a tradition of Jesus warning us about the way a quest for profit adulterates a quest of truth. Invoking a pagan personification of money, he says, "No one can serve two masters: ... You cannot serve God and wealth [Mammon]."[40]

The days of imagining a separation of the life sciences from morality are long gone. We certainly don't want non-scientists to impose a moral code upon science; and yet we scientists are utterly untrained to fashion a scientific morality for the modern age, and we have a ridiculously bad track record when we have previously tried. The best we can do is find an ideological position within evolutionary science that is less stupid and evil than previous attempts to do so. More importantly, we have to convince the public that this isn't the wicked Darwinism of generations past, but a more ideologically benign Darwinism.

CHAPTER THREE

Evolutionary Concepts

In chapter 1, I defined biological evolution as the naturalistic production of difference, and differentiated it from some of its homonyms. Stellar "evolution" for example, involves a transformation of state dictated by physical law. A yellow star will probably eventually become a red giant, because that is what stars do when they have run out of hydrogen atoms to fuse. A star's transformation is highly predictable, and determined by a small number of variables. "Cultural evolution" may involve the direct and conscious production of solutions to environmental problems. And the "evolution" by which an embryo is eventually transformed into a geezer is determined neither by physical law nor by the need to survive, but by the enactment of a genetic program, itself the product of eons of evolution, but which encodes a life cycle.

None of these is what we mean today by "evolution," though. We use the term specifically to refer to the manner by which descendants come to differ from their biological ancestors. Darwin called it "descent with modification." There are, of course, many ways to theorize the relationship between descent and modification. They might be different processes, or different aspects of the same process. The modification might be brief in relation to the descent, or the descent might be brief in relation to the modification. There might be different roles for males and females, or there might be different kinds of responsiveness to the needs set by the environment for survival.

ADAPTATION

For a notable example, take the fit between an organism and its environment, which we call "adaptation." Aristotle believed it was the result of species simply having been built that way. Darwin argued that it was rather the result of a long-term bias in survival and reproduction of organisms that differed slightly from the average, in the direction of a better fit. In other words, that adaptation is the result of history, rather than miracle.

But how does that bias operate in nature? The British polymath Herbert Spencer had been thinking along similar lines, and convinced Darwin that his phrase "survival of the fittest" was effectively synonymous with Darwin's "natural selection." In 1868, Darwin even said so, in *The Variation of Animals and Plants under Domestication:*

> This preservation, during the battle for life, of varieties which possess any advantage in structure, constitution, or instinct, I have called Natural Selection; and Mr. Herbert Spencer has well expressed the same idea by the Survival of the Fittest.[1]

But there is a crucial difference between the two phrases. If only Spencer's "fittest" survive, then the descendant populations can be expected to be very fine-tuned to the environment, since they were not merely fitter, but fittest. The pores of the sieve, so to speak, were very small. Natural selection, on the other hand, makes no claim as to the relative size of the pores. Under extraordinary circumstances, only the fittest may survive, but it is primarily simply the fitter that survive. That necessarily implies a bit more unfitness, or "slop," between the organism and its environment than we might expect if only the fittest were surviving. And sure enough, that question—Just how precisely attuned to the environment are you?—is an unresolved tension in evolution that crops up in unexpected ways.

Biologists since Aristotle haven't doubted the basic fit between what an animal does and where it lives. But that fit was explained by Aristotle by analogy to a human creation, a tool. To Aristotle, a problem is posed: How do I cut this wood? And one makes a saw to solve the problem. That is why the saw cuts wood—it was made to do so. It would be absurd to imagine making a saw for no reason, and then asking what you can do with it, and serendipitously discovering that it is good for cutting wood. Likewise, concluded Aristotle, body parts are made for particular functions, as solutions to environmental problems. The problem came first, and the body part was fashioned to solve it.[2]

Darwinian evolution reverses this relationship: the body part preceded the use, and was merely tweaked to fit. Organisms that could survive a bit longer and more prolifically with a slightly tweaked body part in a particular place became the progenitors of a disproportionate number of descendants, similarly tweaked. The hand, which was once held open to support a monkey's body weight, became modified to suspend an ape's body like a grappling hook, and to support the ape's body on the ground while closed; and later, in people, to hold and manipulate a sharp stone or a pen or a baseball, and not to support the body's weight at all. Aristotle had got it backward; the hand was always there in some form (at least since our ancestors were fish), and it changed over the eons in use and form.

Nevertheless, it is still clear that the fit between an organism and its environment exists. Polar bears are adapted to the arctic, and Gila monsters to the desert. If you study the ecology, behavior, or anatomy of animals, you can't help but see it. If you study the human body in a comparative context, you can't miss the way the human foot is similar to the ape foot, but more stable and rigid, just as its weight-bearing role in human locomotion necessitates.

It is, after all, bodies that adapt. They do so genetically, as in having the right genes turned on at the right time. They also do so developmentally (and irreversibly): the body grows in certain characteristic ways in response to hypoxia or oxygen stress, for example. And they adapt physiologically (and reversibly) as well, as in tanning or shivering or callousing under the stimulation of ultraviolet light or cold or abrasion.

On the other hand, if you study the human genome in a comparative context, all you see is how similar the human genome is to the ape genome. You don't see the feet; for there are no feet in the genome. Nor tans nor shivers nor calluses. There are genes there, not bodies, and it has proven remarkably difficult to match up human genes to human adaptations in any but a small handful of cases. Indeed, it is hard to find adaptation at all reliably in the genome.[3]

The best-known cases of human genetic adaptations to environmental pressure are those to malaria, incorporating a range of blood diseases and other genetic variants, including sickle-cell anemia and thalassemia. But human populations commonly have their own non-adaptive idiosyncrasies—notably, elevated risks of other genetic diseases. These are accidental, not adaptive—for example, porphyria variegata (another blood disease) among white Dutch South Africans, the genetic legacy of a seventeenth-century settler.[4]

Along the lines of sickle-cell anemia, the prevalence of Tay-Sachs (a neurological disease) in the gene pool of Ashkenazi Jews has been suggested as a genetic adaptation affording protection to heterozygotes against either tuberculosis or stupidity.[5] Carriers, in this framework, may be more resistant to tuberculosis, or may instead be a bit smarter than non-carriers. Nevertheless, it is unclear from the population genetics whether selection has operated at all, with over 80 percent of the Tay-Sachs alleles in Ashkenazi Jews being identical, suggestive of a strong "founder effect."[6] After all, the higher prevalence of the disease in French Canadians and Cajuns is interpreted in this way. Carrying the cystic fibrosis allele, more common in northern Europeans than in other populations, has been associated with resistance to many different diseases, all plausible, but none established.[7] While the existence of many alleles causing cystic fibrosis is consistent with an inference of selection, the preponderance of a single one—$\Delta F508$, comprising locally between 40 and 80 percent of the CF alleles in Europe—suggests the complex interplay of stochastic and deterministic forces.[8]

The point is that we ought to be able to distinguish between these alternative explanations, selection and drift. But usually, even with the finest-grained genetic data, we cannot. Usually the best we can do is show that some feature of the genome is more uniform and less diverse than we think it ought to be, and speculate about the reason that its patterns of difference might be so unexpected.

We have two facts about genetics at work here. First, bodies adapt, because they actually interact with environments; and genomes do not, at least not directly. Consequently, where an anatomist can look at the precision engineering of an eye or a hand, the geneticist looking at the genome sees more of a tinkerer at work than an engineer, in the famous metaphor of the French molecular biologist François Jacob.[9] Second, the units of the genome do not map onto the units of the body. We have genes, units of hereditary instruction; and we have elbows, units of the arm—but we don't have "elbow genes." In fact, long after the completion of the Human Genome Project, we still know remarkably little about the production of a four-dimensional (space-filling and maturing) body from a one-dimensional set of instructions (the DNA sequence). We have known for a long time, though—this was known as the "unit-character problem" to an earlier generation[10]—that although the DNA (or genotype) somehow encodes the body (or phenotype), the genetic elements don't correspond to the body parts in any simple way.

Consequently, where an anatomist can see adaptation, and inferentially the invisible hand of natural selection, a geneticist can see sloppiness and wiggle room, produced by a lot of randomness and historical accident.[11] The patterns they see, the questions they ask, and the explanations they invoke differ correspondingly. The geneticist sees a genome in which most DNA changes are neither good nor bad, mutation is a constant but light pressure on the integrity of the system, and DNA sequences are consequently expected to change, indeed to degrade, with some degree of regularity. In fact, the regularity is so much of an expectation that the amount of detectable genetic difference between two species is generally taken as a chronological indication of how long ago their gene pools separated, not of how differently adapted they may or may not have become.[12] When we compare humans and chimpanzees genetically, for example, we see far more readily how similar their genomes are, not how behaviorally, ecologically, demographically, and cognitively different they are. The DNA sequences of two animals that have recently become differently adapted are expected to be very similar, but for the constant pressure of mutation, and the very rare "really good" mutation that actually translates into a physical benefit. Consequently, when examining their genomes, we will expect to find differences, and we explain sequences that are too similar as being constrained by selection, because they are more functionally important than other sections of DNA, where differences are accumulating.

In some cases, DNA sequences that are too different can be identified, but the adaptive story behind them is often thin and insubstantial. The gene called FOXP2 impairs cognitive linguistic competence when mutated. Three coding-sequence mutations differentiate the human gene from the mouse gene, two of which occurred recently in human evolution because even the chimpanzee lacks them. It is certainly a gene involved in language, but is it a language gene? After all, rhesus monkeys and chimpanzees have the same coding sequence, but have quite different vocalizations and cognitive properties. The orangutan has a unique coding-sequence mutation, but no obvious special communicative faculties. And one of the unique human mutations arose in parallel in Carnivora. So one can make a strong case for this gene being nebulously "involved" in cognitive linguistic function, but a considerably weaker case for this gene to be a selectively driven master human language gene, as it is often represented.[13] The problem is that selection occurs on phenotypes, and genotypic data are difficult to translate phenotypically; to think of FOXP2 as a master language gene is to fall into the trap of unit-characters.

The anatomist, on the other hand, focuses on the particular observable differences among species and explains them in terms of the adaptive differences between the species. The similarities require no explanation; one queries not the choice to remain on four legs, made by myriad primate species, but the change to two legs. One does not query the retention of body hair in all other primates, but its loss in one lineage. It is obviously good to be able to speak, but all the species that can't speak seem to make do. We anticipate anatomical stability, which requires no explanation, and we interrogate change, which does require an explanation in terms of Darwinian selection. In contrast, the geneticist expects change, and interrogates stability.

It is hard to overstate the implications of these divergent ways of approaching evolutionary data. Geneticists can see animals that look pretty much the same, but whose genomes are scrambled—for example, gibbons and siamangs. Gibbons and siamangs are both known as "lesser apes," and despite some anatomical distinctions, they are clearly similar kinds of animals, variants on an anatomical theme. Yet gibbon cells have twenty-two pairs of chromosomes, and siamang cells have twenty-five. But that overstates their similarities, for most of the siamang chromosomes cannot even be identified in their gibbon counterparts, because so many rearrangements have arisen between them. Homologous human and chimpanzee chromosomes, by contrast, can be readily matched up and identified almost perfectly. Yet a gibbon sperm with twenty-two chromosomes can fertilize a siamang egg with twenty-five chromosomes, and produce a living hybrid "siabon."[14] It is hard to avoid the conclusion that shuffling the genes around, while leaving them fairly intact, just doesn't interrupt the production of gibbons from their DNA sequences very much. It is a system that cries of slop, not of precision.

Biochemical systems are often characterized by their redundancy, rather than by the efficiency that anatomical systems seem to show. Structurally different proteins can work in other species; form doesn't necessarily follow function so precisely when one deals in biochemicals. Efficiency and adaptation are what you expect if the Spencerian fittest are surviving; wiggle room, redundancy, and slop are what you expect if the Darwinian fit are surviving. Both are likely present, but the point is simply that it is hard to know ahead of time whether any particular feature is actually an "engineered" adaptation or not.

Students of human evolution have repeatedly pointed out that it is unwise to assume that any particular feature is an adaptation, specifically arisen by natural selection, regardless of how useful it seems today, in the absence of strong supporting evidence.[15] Use does not explain origin, since any trait may have multiple uses, which may assume different degrees of importance in particular contexts. This is readily visible in cultural evolution, where (despite the limitations of the analogy to organic evolution) origins are often known and can easily be shown to be different from later primary uses—for example, gunpowder for entertainment, and the Internet as a means of decentralizing computers in the event of nuclear attack. The features indeed found new uses: killing people efficiently and downloading pornography.

Aristotle was right about the saw being made for a specific purpose, but the saw was a carefully chosen cultural feature. If he had chosen something as mundane as clothing, whose purposes include warmth (but we dress even when it's hot out), taboos (certain body parts shouldn't be seen by others), aesthetics, physical protection or comfort, and the communication of a social identity, his error would have been obvious. Old features have multiple uses; some of them may be new, and they may affect our perception of what the feature is primarily used for, which may be quite different from how the feature got started.

The paleontologist Stephen Jay Gould challenged the assumption that any specific biological feature has an origin in natural selection for any one of its particular properties, calling it "Darwinian fundamentalism."[16] Adaptation is more readily seen than established, and living organisms can be surprisingly good at making do with what they have. We know of ways that adaptive, non-adaptive, and even maladaptive features can evolve. The choice of whether to see crafted machinery in nature, as scholars since the Enlightenment have tended to, or bricolage, that is, genetic elements cobbled together into a stable functional state, as modern molecular geneticists do, is an intellectual choice, neither right nor wrong. They are divergent approaches, both of which can be reconciled to evidences of the history of life.

Indeed, this is an intellectual choice that transcends Darwinian evolution, for "adaptationism" goes back to classical times, and to the intellectual themes of natural theology—seeing the wisdom of God in the contrivances of living forms—that Darwin studied in college. We can study what a feature *does*, and we can study *how it got there*, but to ask *what it is for* is to decorate the scientific question with a lot of metaphysical accessories that it just doesn't need. To ask what it is for is to assume that there is a reason for it—a deterministic, selective regime for the feature; a particular optimal solution to a problem. But actually, there may be no reasons for some things, just naturalistic causes and uses, and a lot of random noise; life may be more like clothes than like saws.

SPECIES

The fundamental contribution of population genetics to evolutionary theory is its ability to reduce evolution to the transformation of gene pools, and to reduce the transformation of gene pools to a small number of processes, with mathematically predictable effects. This was accomplished by the middle of the twentieth century and came to be known as the "synthetic theory" of evolution. Mutations make new alleles for populations; Darwinian natural selection makes populations different in ways that track the environment, and result in a fit between the gene pool and its surroundings; genetic drift makes populations randomly different, not tracking the environment; and gene flow or interbreeding makes two gene pools less distinct and more homogeneous. Two things were sacrificed, however: bodies and species. By exchanging bodies for genotypes and species for gene pools, midcentury biologists deferred two important questions of physiology for future generations. First, what is the relationship between genotypes and bodies; how reliable a predictor of the latter is the former? And second, how do animals come to identify one another as a part of the same species?

The great evolutionary biologists of the mid-twentieth century evaded these problems by defining them out of existence. By reducing species to gene pools, so they could be mathematically formalized, we made animals essentially automatic outgrowths of their genotypes. By failing to problematize the body itself, then, we failed to problematize the origin of adaptive novelties, the things that allow us to survive and reproduce; it was kept as an article of faith that genetic changes somehow create new bodies. In its most extreme version, Richard Dawkins famously argued that genes are the only significant evolutionary units, and bodies themselves are simply "gigantic lumbering robots."[17]

One of the cardinal tenets of Darwinism is the continuity between the patterns and processes that differentiate animal varieties or breeds from one another, and those that differentiate animal species from one another. And Darwin was certainly mostly right about that: higher taxonomic categories (like orders of mammals) generally have the same kinds of differences that lower taxonomic categories (like genera of African monkeys) have—in body form, coloration, behavior, chromosome number and shape, DNA sequence—but more of them, and to a greater extent. The differences among breeds of pigeons or dogs or cows are fewer and smaller, but are the same kinds of differences as those that differentiate pigeons from doves, dogs from bears, and cows from antelopes. There is one point of departure, however. Animals of the same species recognize others of their species as potential mates or competitors for mates. Sometimes they try to mate and breed with other species and fail, but usually they don't even try. Cats mate with other cats, not with dogs or cows.

There is some biological unit, call it a species for the sake of simplicity, within which animals see each other as potential mates or competitors for mates, and outside of which they don't. In three dimensions, they constitute clusters of reproductively compatible organisms; in four dimensions, they are diverging lineages.[18] Consequently, the production of new evolutionary lineages, or speciation, must entail the development of mate-recognition systems:[19] in the case of flies, doing the right dance or having the right pheromone; in the case of chimpanzees, pink swellings of the female genitalia; in the case of humans, looking good. The diverse things that turn people on—power, fame, a great body, flattery, fantasy, erogeny—just aren't meaningful to a chimpanzee. And swollen pink genitalia don't work on us. At least on me, anyway.

The classical assumption of theoretical population genetics is that the accumulation of difference somehow causes the multiplication of lineages, that differences of genetic quantity eventually translate into differences of evolutionary quality. Population genetics showed how to model the transformation of a gene pool, but there is more here than just transformation, there is multiplication. At some point populations of animals become so different from one another, or so different in particular ways, that they become separately evolving lineages. By the 1940s, evolutionary biologists had begun to examine the process of diversification itself, in genetic, geographic, and temporal dimensions.[20] And as we will see in chapter 4, by the 1980s mainstream evolutionary biologists were appreciating the limitations of the reductive definition of evolution as "changes in gene frequencies through time" and had come to acknowledge that even a minimal definition of evolution had to incorporate diversification, the production of new species, and not merely the transformation of old ones.[21]

Philosophically, this entails recognizing that a species is not a class of animals defined by the possession of common attributes, but an elemental unit of animal history composed of interrelated parts. The analogy would be to the composition of your body as made up of just cells, but different from the contents of a flask of cells in a biology laboratory. The cells of your body compose you by virtue of their organizational, relational, or epigenetic aspects,[22] in spite of being genetically identical to one another; organisms make species likewise by virtue of their relationships to one another. That is to say, a cell begins and ends, reproduces and interacts with an environment. So does a body. And so does a species. It begins, it goes extinct, it speciates, and it occupies an ecological niche. And it is composed of organisms that relate to one another in specific ways, analogous to the way in which organisms are composed of cells that relate to one another in specific ways—differently from the contents of a large flask. Cell biologists had long acknowledged these hierarchical relationships in the natural world;[23] and the idea of hierarchy yields a valuable alternative to the reductive view that holds organisms to be "just" genotypes, evolution to be "just" changes in gene frequencies, and species to be "just" gene pools.

It's a sloppy central concept, though, the species—reminiscent of "culture" in anthropology and "gene" in genetics. It can mean different things in different contexts, and is most applicable only among the most familiar kinds of creatures—namely, sexually reproducing animals. And yet, it clearly represents something real, a natural unit of animals partaking of a common gene pool, with a genetic, ecological, and historical existence separate and distinct from other comparable units. It is this knowledge, what kind of animal you are, that establishes the limits of the gene pool, and circumscribes a species in space and time—at least in theory. In practice, it is always a bit more complicated, with biological issues like intermediate states of interfertility, and cultural concerns sometimes trumping evolutionary genetics.[24]

PHYLOGENY AS ANCESTRY

Paleontology works with less information than the study of living species does, without physiology or social behavior or genetics, with the principal exception being the study of DNA from recently extinct animals. But paleontology does have one set of data that the study of living species lacks, namely, time depth.

This allows it to ask questions that would be otherwise invisible. How rapid is the process of speciation, relative to the duration of the species? What is the role of unpredictable and non-adaptive processes, such as mass extinctions, on the history of life?[25]

The latter question actually hits at some existential philosophical questions. Are we here for a reason? Is there something special about our species? Here again, there are epistemic choices. On the one hand, Stephen Jay Gould argued that the history of life was full of randomness, like history is. If Hitler hadn't invaded Russia, you might be reading this passage in German, or not at all. If the dinosaurs hadn't died out 65 million years ago, primates probably wouldn't have evolved, and again, you wouldn't be here. That suggests that our existence as a species is historically precarious and not in any sense inevitable. On the other hand, some biologists point to the ubiquity of parallel evolution in nature. Given that flight arose in insects, reptiles, birds, and mammals, these biologists ask, Why wouldn't intelligence evolve eventually in another group of species?[26]

On the third hand, a lot of species haven't evolved—species with three hands, for example, or telekinesis or invisibility or the Midas touch. Is it really true that if we wait long enough, eventually a species will arise that will shit gold ingots? No, your imagination is not the limiting factor in evolution. The fact that something has never evolved is not a good guide to whether it could ever evolve, and the fact that something evolved once may not be a good guide to whether it could arise again. This view of course is also a bucket of cold water on exobiology, which presumes that life could/did evolve elsewhere, and that the evolution of an intelligent technological lineage, which took 3 billion years to happen here just once, would happen somewhere else, in some kind of recognizable form.[27]

Watch the skies! (For the weather, not for space aliens—because the weather is all that's up there.)

To return to reality, what about the nature of species—are they stable through time, or constantly changing? That was the question posed by paleontologists Niles Eldredge and Stephen Jay Gould in a series of papers in the 1970s and 1980s. Although they gave it a highfalutin name, punctuated equilibria, it was rooted in querying a basic assumption about the nature of species.[28] Are they constantly adapting to constantly changing environmental circumstances, or do they remain more or less as they began, until another new and slightly better-adapted descendant species comes to supplant them? In either case, we are describing the same set of data, animal A alive at one time, and animal B, very similar, alive at a later time. Obviously we have to connect the dots, but what is the geometry of the connection? Are A and B representatives of different species? A straight line from A to B would imply not just that A evolved into B, but that it did so in a particular way, gradually and by indiscernible increments. The alternative is that species A was stable through time, and its successor, species B (assuming they were different species), was also stable through time, but that the descent of B from A was brief relative to the longevity of species A and B. A good analogy might be the nine-month human gestation relative to an eighty-year life span: assuming that you remain a single entity from cradle to grave, it took a relatively very short time to make you.

What the punctuated equilibria controversy highlighted is that the nature and pattern of ancestral and descendant relationships are not discovered; they are imposed. (A common misconception about punctuated equilibria is that it purports to explain the "gaps" between higher taxa, like reptiles and mammals, or between fish and tetrapods, or between whales and other artiodactyls. Those skeletal transitions are known, to greater or lesser extents, in the fossil record in genera such as *Morganucodon, Ambulocetus,* and *Tiktaalik,* but that's not what punctuated equilibria is about   it's about the nature of the relationship between two closely related forms, and the nature of species.)

Patterns of similarity among living beings are most plausibly explained by a process of common descent. Nevertheless, living species constitute a trivially small and non-random subset of all species. Extinct species, however, do not leave a trail of descent; they leave a trail of similarities, which must be transformed into a narrative of descent.[29] The properties of an organism may fossilize, but the relationships between organisms do not; they have to be inferred. So, is an organism in species A literally the ancestor of an organism in species B? Alas, we can probably never know, but what we do know suggests that it's pretty unlikely. Of course, lots of individual organisms don't themselves reproduce. Moreover, since (1) patterns of ancestry are invariably inferred, not discovered, and (2) the sampling of extinct species is very poor, it follows that we rarely, if ever, can discover a particular species that is literally the ancestor of another, much less that an individual in one species is an ancestor of an individual in another species. Instead we say, "This evolved into that" when we really mean, "Something rather like this evolved into that." The statement ("This evolved into that") is a shorthand; it is precise without necessarily being accurate.

Substituting precision for accuracy, with embarrassing results, is not altogether unknown in science. For decades, cell biologists had been trying to count the number of chromosomes in a human cell that is about to divide. It was, however, rather like trying to count the strands in a bowl of spaghetti. It was clearly a number in the high forties—but rather than say, "a number in the high forties," they went with a particular number in the high forties, namely, forty-eight, because in 1923, the most respected researcher in the field said that's what he thought the number was. And biology textbooks from the 1920s through the 1950s routinely told students that there are forty-eight chromosomes in a human cell. Researchers, knowing the precise answer, routinely convinced themselves that they could see all forty-eight chromosomes. But the precise answer was not the correct one, because in 1956, with technological improvements, scientists began to see only forty-six chromosomes in each normal human cell.[30]

And remember, all they were doing is counting.

RELATEDNESS

The issue here is the relationship between things, as distinct from the properties of the things themselves. If A looks a lot like B, and lived earlier than B, and you are committed to a naturalistic explanation for the history of life, then it is certainly quite reasonable to infer that something like A evolved into something like B, even if A itself didn't exactly evolve into B itself.

That's boring. It was even boring to write. But "A evolved into B" is an origin myth. It is a narrative about the relationship between A and B, extrapolated from their properties and relative chronology.[31] It is a narrative about ancestry and descent, which humans are always interested in, because narratives of ancestry and descent tell them who they are and where they fit in, in a world of close relatives, distant relatives, and strangers.

Those narratives are always important and meaningful. What do the actor Kirk Douglas and the anthropologist Ashley

Montagu have in common? They both tried to put a little bit of distance between themselves and their ancestry by renaming themselves in less "ethnically marked" ways.[32] In a world where your ancestry may be held against you, you may need to create a new ancestry for yourself. In early Christian communities the desire to establish Jesus as a true King of Israel seemed to necessitate tracking his descent from the biblical King David. And different Christian communities tracked that ancestry in different ways. Consequently, two of the Gospels we now have, Matthew and Luke, do precisely that—they track the ancestry of Jesus back to King David but they do so in different numbers of generations, and with almost entirely different names.[33]

Narratives of ancestry are invariably mythic, for a simple statistical reason. Every ancestor had two parents; the number of your ancestors in every generation increases exponentially. Barely 300 years ago, you had thousands of lineal ancestors. To make sense of such chaos, what human groups do is to privilege certain ancestors over others, The fact that you are a lineal descendant of George Washington is far more important than the fact that you are also a lineal descendant of thousands of his contemporaries, who aren't very important, or at least not as important as he is. And frankly, the chance that what little DNA you actually share with your lineal ancestor George Washington was actually his best DNA, is pretty small.

Ancestry, then, is an origin myth. It takes the world of biological data and emphasizes some things, invents others, and relates the present to the past in a meaningful way. Each way of doing so is constrained by cultural rules—and evolution, being a scientific origin myth, is constrained by the assumptions of naturalism, empiricism, and rationalism that bound modern science. And of course, there are other ways of understanding ancestry than the biological or scientific; and these may intersect in weird ways.

For example, no sensible person thinks that molecular genomics yields any support to biblical literalism or creationism, but consider these two sets of facts. First, genomics is a different kind of science, in which money is often at stake, because it is highly corporatized. Second, the facts it produces are also consequently a different class of facts—they are bio-cultural facts. Now you have the tools to make some sense of recreational ancestry testing.

Recreational ancestry testing is a thriving business. A company such as "rootsforreal.com" can tell you if you have the Y chromosome of Moses. To wit:

> The priestly caste of the Cohanim are thought to have the same Y chromosome as the biblical Moses, because Aaron, Moses' brother, founded this priesthood, whose duties traditionally pass from father to son. The Cohanim Y type identified in groundbreaking analysis by the team of Prof. David Goldstein and colleagues agrees with the biblical tradition, and a simple Y test using our database search can confirm whether a Cohen male indeed carries the Cohen Y type.[34]

This is independent of the fact that Moses is as much a mythic character as King Arthur and Odysseus, although if anyone claimed to be able to test whether you have the DNA of wily Odysseus, you would think they were crazy. Especially if you consult your Bible, and learn from Genesis 5 of the patrilineage connecting Adam and Noah, from Genesis 11 of the patrilineage connecting Noah and Abraham, and Exodus 6, which extends the patrilineage to Moses and Aaron. Yes, this is not just the Y chromosome of the Lawgiver, but the Y chromosome of Adam as well.

Shhhhh. Don't tell the creationists.

What on earth is going on here?

It's about the significance and marketability of ancestry. Let us add some more bio-cultural facts. First, scientists are more willing to accept Exodus literally than Genesis. I'm not sure why. Second, people tend to be genetically more similar to people with the same surnames (in this case, Cohen or its derivatives) than to random people. Third, people who consider themselves to be part of the priestly lineage in Judaism are disproportionately named "Cohen" or a derivative. Fourth, the story is relatively innocuous; hence we can label the consumer product as "recreational." Fifth, the Jews a have a complicated demographic history, even a mythic one, with ancient origin stories from Palestine, Egypt, and Babylonia. Sixth, sure, there might be other ways of explaining the data, but this interpretation—that the Y-chromosome configuration held by most people named Cohen is the descendant of the Y chromosome of the original high priest Aaron, who had the same Y chromosome as Moses, because they were brothers—might be true.

There is, of course, real science at work here.[35] The initial paper was published in *Nature*, the leading science journal in the world, and actually began, "According to biblical accounts, the Jewish priesthood was established about 3,300 years ago ." My hat is off to anyone with the chutzpah to start a paper in *Nature*, "According to biblical accounts . . ." But there is DNA sequencing, and plausible analysis. Now it could be that they have discovered the Y chromosome of Moses and Adam; or alternatively, it could be that they have discovered that a sample of Jews with similar surnames tend to be genetically alike, and that happens to be the Y-chromosome configuration that most of them have by virtue of the complexities of Jewish demographic history. Of course, if it really were the latter, who would be interested in buying the test at $300 a pop?

So, never mind that the leading science journal in the world published a paper that begins with the assumption that the biblical characters are real (although perhaps without their participation in the miraculous plagues, manna from heaven, and parting of the sea)—and nobody batted an eye. Imagine if, instead of Moses and Aaron, they had actually claimed to have discovered the Y chromosome of Noah and Abraham—in which case the Science Police would have rung alarms in every conceivable forum. (And they actually could have made that claim from their data, given the biblical genealogical connections noted above.) The point is that this is about business and mythology and genomics simultaneously, and you can't disentangle them. We like to think that genetics or genomics is an uncultural, purely objective scientific view of ancestry, but it isn't—as the 1995 classic, *The DNA Mystique: The Gene as Cultural Icon,* by the sociologist Dorothy Nelkin and historian Susan Lindee famously explored. This is science, all right, but it is very cultural science; for this is about ancestry, and ancestry involves the privileged relations among people. And it is precisely those relations that are constructed and anthropological, not given by nature.[36]

FAMILIES

Each of us has an inheritance from our ancestors. That inheritance, however, is complex, consisting of both organic (living cellular matter) and non-organic (traditions, silverware) features. The organic heritage bounds and differentiates us as individuals: everyone's DNA is slightly different. It also bounds and differentiates us as a species: every species's DNA is slightly different. In between the organism and the species, however, our biological patterns and distinctions are far more subtle.

Groups of humans are similar to, yet different from, their neighbors. We aren't like our neighbors; we do things differently, in a more civilized, sensitive, spiritual way. We define them in opposition to ourselves, we don't like their ways, or their mode of speech, and yet we trade with them, in a pinch we may rely on them, we may even fall in love with them. It's a peculiarly human way to think: we imagine others as similar or different according to shifting, situation-specific, historically produced ideas about what kinds of similarities and differences matter. Certainly the most fundamental idea of similarity and difference resides in the decision about who is a member of our family and who is not. That decision creates the available choices for sexual and marriage partners, given the broad taboo on having sex with a nuclear family member. And yet, that decision about who is a part of our family is subject to extraordinary levels of flexibility, as social anthropologists have documented extensively.

In other words, we need to know who is a member of our family and who is not, but because the family is constituted from compromises between lineal blood relationships (parenthood, generally speaking) and legal bonds (marriage, residency, and adoption), the boundaries of the family are often quite fuzzy. So we sharpen them with our special rules, which may not map particularly well onto our genetic relationships, but at least we now know what to do.

And the same problem recurs at a higher level. Our family is "especially close relatives," who are segregated by definition from a broader category, "relatives." And yet "relatives" is not an unproblematic natural category either, since biologically, we are all related. Somehow we also have to decide that a second cousin is a relative, but a twentieth cousin is not. Or even more arbitrarily, that one twentieth cousin (sharing your last name or a critical bit of your genome) might be a relative, and another twentieth cousin is not. These are units built up from nature/culture—the family, the kin-group, the race, the nation, the species—bounded in part or in varying degrees by natural properties, and in part by imaginary fences.

Historically, narratives of human origins have incorporated narratives of human diversity (the former presumably explaining the latter), but these scientific narratives of contemporary difference have always been co-produced by the author's social and political circumstances. Thus, Darwin's *Descent of Man* (1871) is far more a text of Victorian social prejudices than his earlier *Origin of Species* (1859), which famously omitted all but the most oblique reference to people, and is consequently far more readable all these years later.

CLADES AND RHIZOMES

The cultural aspects of ancestry, even in evolution, come out in another interesting way. Since the cessation of gene flow classically implies a new species and a new evolving lineage, it is classically assumed that, above species level, gene pools can only diverge from one another, since they can't get more similar through gene flow or interbreeding. There might be some superficial similarities emerging when distinct lineages cope with certain environmental challenges in convergent ways, but the fact is that bats can't mate with birds, and dolphins can't mate with sharks. Consequently the most famous image of evolution is as a tree, its branches ever diverging from one another.[37]

That is a useful image for macroevolution. For microevolution, however, we must look to another part of the tree—to its root system, Roots, unlike branches, are not always separating from one another. Roots may often fuse with one another, to create a connected network whose individual paths may be very difficult to delineate. They're like populations of organisms, evolving somewhat separately, but still connected by gene flow. While they become distinct in minor ways, nevertheless like Michael Corleone trying to escape from the Mafia, they keep getting pulled back in.

There is an important difference between the two systems. A group of distinct species who are each other's closest relatives is a clade; and a network of subspecific populations is a rhizome. Within a clade, there is a simple answer to the question, Which are really the closest relatives? The closest relatives are the species that shared a common ancestor most recently. But for a rhizomatic network, which may resemble a train trellis or a capillary system more than the branches of a tree, there is no simple answer, since sharing recent common ancestry is not the only variable; it gets combined with how much and how recently there has been interbreeding with other parts of the network.

In principle, there may actually be no answer to the "closest relatives" question in a system that isn't constantly diverging, as species are. In practice, however, you can program a computer to answer a different question—Which are most similar?—and draw a rhizomatic system as if it were a tree. The results might then look like they had a great deal more evolutionary validity than they actually do.

Thus, a population genetics project might pose a question about whether, "for example, the Irish are more closely related to the Spaniards or to the Swedes."[38] And they can get an answer. But that answer will be dependent upon who is actually taken to represent the nationalities in question (are we sampling the real Swedes of today, or the Swedes we imagine of 500 years ago?), their demographic expansions and contractions, and the particular algorithms used to construct the tree—as well as the nature and extent of gene flow, and the divergences that actually frame the question. The idea that a tree would represent only the last of these is at best a very hopeful one.

A parallel problem exists when the "closest relatives" question is applied to things like languages and human artifacts. The issue is the imposition of a tree-like structure on histories that are basically not tree-like, an altogether too-common practice, often concealed by appeals to evolution and technology.

But the bigger problem remains its application to human populations, and the casual interpretation of the resulting tree of statistically generated similarity as a phylogenetic tree of history. And perhaps the most unusual situation exists when we can't tell whether the units we are clustering are species (in which case we might well be reconstructing relationships of descent) or subspecies and local populations (in which case we probably aren't). If we "split" the human fossil lineages, we make it look as if we are indeed dealing with species, and the cladistic analysis ought to work: a tree ought to be a good approximation of a branching history. But if we "lump" those fossils, all bets are off—because we might be dealing with the Irish-Spanish-Swedish problem, except over much larger ranges of space and time.

The fossils recently discovered at Dmanisi, Georgia, suggest that we are indeed dealing with strongly rhizomatic relationships in the human fossil record, back to nearly 2 million years ago.[39] Several anthropologists had suggested this over the years—Earnest Hooton invoking the metaphor of a capillary system; Franz Weidenreich and, later, Frederick Hulse invoking the train trellis; and others invoking a root system or mesh net[40]—and it looks like they might just have been right. How you allocate the fossils taxonomically is how you begin to make human evolution into a story—whether you narrate human evolution as linear, with very few species, culminating in our own; or as bushy, with many species, and all but one having gone extinct. The line and the bush—and their intermediates, bushy lines—are each narratives of human evolution, and understanding that narrative aspect is central to thinking clearly about human evolution.

Human evolution, then, is a theory of kinship—or a set of theories about kinship and is not fully accessible through zoology. Theories of human relatedness and descent at all levels are bio-cultural theories, not strictly natural ones.

CHAPTER FOUR

How to Think about Evolution Non-reductively

Since the middle of the twentieth century, the rigorous mathematical formalism of population genetics has fostered a reductive view of the evolutionary processes. We could reduce species to a pool of their genes, a person to their genotype, and evolution to a change in allele frequencies over time. The reductive view from population genetics reached its climax in *Adaptation and Natural Selection* by George C. Williams (1966) and *The Selfish Gene* by Richard Dawkins (1976).

There were, of course, minority voices to remind us that species are not just fields of genes; that a living four-dimensional organism is often not predictable from a genotype; and that evolution encompasses a lot more than just changes in allele frequencies. Cell biologists, for example, had long grappled with the fact that life is hierarchically organized. Even though a human being is composed of just cells and their products, a human body is organized cells, and understanding the nature of that organization is critical to understanding the body. By the same token a species is not simply a cluster of animals, but a special kind of cluster of animals—those that see themselves some-how as potential mates or competitors for mates. Once again, the nature of the organization of the units is what creates the higher-order structure.

The evolutionary biologist Ernst Mayr had challenged the reductive paradigm, calling it "beanbag genetics" in a famous 1959 paper.[1] Likewise the population geneticist Richard Lewontin advocated for different "units of selection" in a famous 1970 paper. By the 1980s, a mainstream reaction against the reductive view of evolution was under way, spearheaded by the paleontologist Stephen Jay Gould.[2]

In challenging the reductive view of evolution, the midcentury ideas of the brilliant developmental geneticist Conrad Waddington were rediscovered (he died in 1975). Waddington had been an unapologetic holist in an age of reductionism, and conceptualized evolution within a hierarchical and cybernetic framework. His invocation of biological levels of organization and interactions among them was more complex than the standard reductive model, and perhaps left his contemporaries a bit intimidated. Nevertheless, it is now clear that Waddington's systemic idea of evolution is a lot closer to reality than the alternative, and provides a valuable framework for thinking about the evolutionary processes that have produced the familiar modern human condition.[3]

Waddington envisioned a hierarchy of process, all ultimately accruing to the production of genetic differences between ancestors and descendants.[4] Waddington, however, centralized organisms rather than alleles. His model began with organisms, but not as static animals—rather, with the "point that the organisms undergoing the process of evolution are themselves processes."[5] Waddington deliberately introduces agency into animals, by noting that they choose where to live, and in so doing, they modify their habitat simply by being in it. He called this relationship between the organism and the environment "The Exploitive System." As it grows and matures, the organism is faced with certain stresses that test its ability to adapt and survive. He called these developmental potentials "The Epigenetic System" and the ability to survive and breed by developing a particular way in that particular setting, "The Natural Selective System." Finally (and significantly, for its trailing place in the processual evolutionary hierarchy), Waddington called attention to the modification of those "selected potentialities" via mutation in "The Genetic System."

The salient features of Waddington's view of evolution are the recognitions that (1) the conceptual units in evolution have overlapping hierarchical relations; (2) organisms do not reside in niches, but partly make them; (3) organisms are not always adults, but grow and develop in response to the particular circumstances of their lives; and (4) organisms vary physiologically in their ability to make those developmental responses, which in turn is an important component of their relative survival and reproduction.

What follows is an expansion and modification of Waddington's systemic theory of evolution. We will think of the processes of human evolution here in terms of five nested systems: the genetic, the developmental, the exploitive, the cultural, and the natural selective (fig. 1). These systems are not bounded or discrete; they interact with one another and bleed into one another. Seeing evolution in this way, however, helps to make the point that the classical reductive model is really only the starting point of an understanding of evolution.

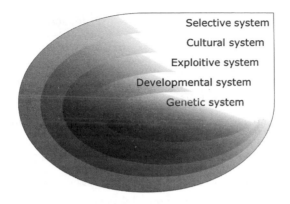

Figure 1. Hierarchical evolutionary systems.

THE GENETIC SYSTEM

This system is the cellular basis of evolution, the creation of new genetic variation. With the discovery of the structure of DNA in 1953, and subsequently of genome structure, we now know the most fundamental ways in which heritable changes are produced. They are produced by changes in genes, which are units of function within the genome. The genome is made of DNA, and the genes are islands, embedded in oceans of DNA with either no function or very limited and cryptic function.

Only about 2 percent of the genome is actually functional in the classic genic sense of "coding for proteins" through an RNA intermediary. Somewhat more is obscurely functional, being transcribed into RNA, but not actually expressed in any obvious way physically. But most of the genome lies between genes; or lies within genes, and is deleted from the RNA transcript before protein translation. Consequently it has traditionally been regarded as being of very limited value or utility, although the possibility exists that the cell has uses for some of it that we do not yet see or understand.[6]

Two lines of evolutionary evidence converged to produce this understanding of the genome. By the 1960s, human diabetes was found to be treatable by injections of insulin derived from a cow or pig pancreas, despite the fact that there are some structural differences among the hormone molecules. Far from being precisely attuned to cow physiology, the bovine insulin molecule works well in humans, which in turn seems to imply a great deal of slop in the genetic system. Discoveries such as these suggested empirically that the genetic system ought to be best understood without the assumption that it has been precisely engineered by natural selection, that is to say, as "non-Darwinian evolution."[7]

Further, the genomes can be scrambled without apparently compromising the production of organisms, as we noted in chapter 3 with the example of the "siabon." On the basis of early genomic data like these, the molecular biologist François Jacob famously argued that genetic evolution acted not like an engineer, but like a tinkerer, drawing inspiration from the anthropologist Claude Lévi-Strauss's work on mythology.[8] The storyteller, said Lévi-Strauss, does not compose an optimal story from scratch, but rather, cobbles together available motifs and suitable themes, tries them out, sees what parts work well together, and consequently assembles a story that will be familiar and resonant for the audience, without necessarily being efficient, brief, or perfectly suited. In a similar fashion, argued Jacob, nature works with genetic systems that are functional, redundant, and suboptimal, and transforms them into other novel systems with those properties. Thus, at least from the standpoint of genetics, we should see evolution metaphorically not as an engineer, but as a *bricoleur,* or tinkerer. Both the gibbon and siamang genomes work; they just do so with radically redeployed genes.[9]

So DNA is not like a blueprint, despite the hype for the Human Genome Project in the 1990s, in a critical way. Most DNA is irrelevant to the production of an organism; you can scramble it up, or even delete chunks of it, often with no apparent ill effects. DNA is not fine-tuned or precisely engineered, or well adapted; it simply gets the job of building an organism done—and there are a lot of genetic ways of getting to the same end point.

Mutations are changes to the DNA in a cell, and usually they don't matter at all, and simply accumulate in species over time. That is because of the limited functionality of most of the DNA; change it, and it doesn't make you better or worse. The changes that do occur in functional genes are more likely to make you worse than to improve you. The reason is simply that over the course of the eons of the history of life, our genomes have evolved to produce bodies that function. Random changes are not likely to improve them, any more than random changes to functioning machines are likely to improve them. That is why mutations give you cancer, not X-ray vision. Nevertheless, what differentiates organic "machinery" from the engineered products of human labor is the degree of slop that we find in nature, as opposed to the efficient human engineering of machinery. Randomly change the blueprint and the machine will simply not run as it was designed to, even if it is not supposed to run at maximum efficiency.

Consequently, when we compare DNA across species, we almost always find more differences in non-coding, intergenic DNA than in coding, genic DNA. And within genes, we find more differences across species in DNA regions or sites that do not change the protein products than in places that do change the protein products. Nevertheless this kind of comparison measures only one kind of mutation—nucleotide substitutions, the change of an A, G, C, or T in DNA for one of the other letters. Since the 1980s, it has become clear that there are many more ways to change the DNA—for example, by inserting or deleting small tandemly repetitive DNA sequences, or larger movable DNA sequences, or by using the DNA in one gene as a template to alter the sequence of a gene beside it.

The ultimate result is simply that new DNA sequences are produced, which may have some effect upon the physiology or anatomy of the organism, the things that actually interact with the environment, which of course the genetic system does not.

THE DEVELOPMENTAL SYSTEM

By the late 1930s, Waddington was distinguishing between genetic differences, which exist in the DNA sequences from person to person, and epigenetic differences, which differ from cell to cell within the same person, in spite of genetic uniformity. Both patterns of difference are stably inherited: aside from rare somatic mutations, a body develops mitotically from a fertilized egg, while retaining the same genotype over the course of the life span; and muscle cells give rise to other muscle cells, not to nerve cells. The nature of the epigenetic system proved more elusive than the genetic system, however, and the rise of molecular biology in the 1960s and the Human Genome Project in the 1980s left the question of epigenetics behind. But at some point there is a fundamental difference between a human being and a 170-pound flask of human cells. The nature of that difference, and its role in evolution, is the study of epigenetics, or as Waddington called it, "the causal analysis of development."[10]

How do cells make bodies? By turning certain arrays of genes on and off, and making sure they stay that way in descendant cells. The biochemistry of epigenetics lies in the regulation of genes—specializing the cells and organizing them, and in the ways in which that information is transmitted to daughter cells after cell division. The crucial aspect of epigenetics is that two cells with identical DNA sequences can be programmed to look and act differently, and that programming can persist across cell generations and across organismal generations. Moreover, since the conditions of life can affect the epigenetic programming of cells, it now seems possible that those conditions of life (i.e., the environment) can have an effect upon the cellular development of the body, and that this in turn can produce a fit between the organism and environment that is independent of its DNA sequence, and that can be stably inherited as if it were genetic. Thus the body can be seen as reactive and dynamic, rather than as passive and static.

Epigenetics emphasizes two features of the body that the DNA sequence misses. The first is adaptability, the property of a body to adjust developmentally to environmental insults.[11] We noted some examples of this feature in chapter 3: hypoxia, tanning, and callousing, for example. The second is canalization, the property of a body to find a "normal" way to develop, in spite of environmental or genetic variation. In a famous 1956 experiment, Waddington subjected fruit flies to a chemical interruption of their development, and found that most of them died, but a few of them survived, while developing a weird condition: a second thorax. This wasn't a new mutation (which would only have originated in a single fly, and there is a mutation that mimics this condition), but a different pathway of development, stimulated by the presence of ether in the fly egg's atmospheric environment. Waddington artificially selected for those flies that were able to make this developmental adjustment, and soon had a strain of flies that could consistently develop the bithorax phenotype under the environmental stimulation of the ether. Waddington had successfully selected for the physiological property of adaptability; he had a line of flies whose physiology had allowed them to survive by developing very weirdly when appropriately stimulated—rather than simply dying. Then he began to breed and select those flies under conditions of lower ether concentrations, and soon he had a strain of flies that developed the bithorax phenotype without ether at all. He had selected for canalization, so that the flies had found a "new normal."[12]

This appeared to mimic the pattern of Lamarckian inheritance, or the inheritance of acquired characteristics, but Waddington explained the pattern by a strictly Mendelian process. The genes involved were not genes for phenotypes, as the reductive population geneticists saw things, but rather, genes for the ability to physiologically adjust. In the first phase of the experiment, he was selecting for genes (which have still not been isolated) that allowed the fly to develop weirdly, rather than simply to die in the toxic conditions (adaptability). And in the second phase, he was selecting for genes that permitted the weird phenotype to become the normal one (canalization).

How might these ideas be applicable to humans? Consider our most fundamental feature, bipedality. Under the reductive model, where genes code directly for phenotypes, we have often imagined bipedalism emerging gradually from the successive fixation of uprightness mutations, as a quadrupedal ancestor at a 45-degree angle had mutations that allowed its descendants to walk at a 60-degree angle, who then had mutations that allowed their descendants to rise to 70 degrees, and eventually to perfect

90-degree verticality. And all this presumably was accompanied by the gradual accumulation of mutations that altered the pelvis, knees, legs, spine, and cranial base in parallel.

The problem is that all of those intermediate states never existed. They are certainly not evident in the fossil record. Apes usually walk quadrupedally, but sometimes do walk bipedally. They do it over short distances and clumsily, but discretely, and both modes are part of their locomotor repertoire. They can sometimes walk on two feet, although not for long, when they want to. It stands to reason that our own ancestors could do it also. Consequently, we must think of the evolution of bipedalism not as the acquisition of a brand-new feature, but as a transition from a facultative to an obligate manner of walking. That is, an ancestor that could walk bipedally, essentially chose to do more of it, and now has descendants that can do nothing but.

But now, instead of an empirical problem, we have a theoretical problem, for that is just not supposed to happen. Choices that you make in your life can't get into your DNA and be passed on to your descendants. You can choose to root for the Red Sox, but your children might root for the Yankees. You inherit your DNA, but you don't modify it. It's like bodily mutilations. If you cut the tails off of fifty generations of mice, the fifty-first generation has tails as long as the first. Why? Because you changed their tails, not their DNA. How might the choice to walk upright more frequently have occurred genetically? Waddington's ideas are useful here.

An ancestor that began to walk upright more frequently would have considerably different stresses placed upon its skeleton. Its center of gravity would lie atop its pelvis, rather than ahead of the pelvis; its feet would be supporting its full body weight, rather than just its rear weight, for example. These stresses would result in developmental modifications of the body, such as the curvature of the lumbar region of the spine—like the bithorax fruit flies, but less bizarre. Some early humans would be better able to make these skeletal adjustments than others—this would be natural selection for adaptability. Subsequently, natural selection for "the new normal"—canalization—would facilitate the developmental appearance of these features. There might well be tweaking to be done, in the fixation of mutations affecting body proportions, for example; and further, bipedalism is crucially a learned behavior in humans (see below)—but to model it effectively as a genetic process, we need to think of it as a developmental system, rather than as a static set of mutations-for-traits.[13] Indeed, a parallel argument can be made for the locomotor transition from fish to tetrapod.[14]

The relationship between the genetic system and the epigenetic or developmental system is also highly political. In chapter I, we observed that the punch line of the very first textbook of Mendelian genetics was that "the creature is not made, but born." Whether true or not, it certainly has considerable bio-political content. You inherit your genes from your ancestors, so are you any more than their genes? Those at the top of a hereditary aristocracy would certainly like to think not. If you are simply a reconstitution of your ancestors, then the possession of a noble pedigree is all you need to establish your superiority to the rest of the world. This mode of thought has always been there in science: by the end of the nineteenth century, biology was very polarized between two bio-political views. Followers of the biologist August Weismann called themselves "neo-Darwinians" and held that the germ cells comprise a link between the generations, and the body (Greek, *soma*) is simply a cellular dead end. Thus, through the "continuity of the germ-plasm" you are simply a reconstituted product of your ancestors, an argument that of course resonated strongly with political conservatives in fin-de-siècle Europe. But if you are not simply a reconstitution of your ancestors, then what else are you made of? Scientists with left-leaning political views found other things to study that shaped human existence: notably, culture, parenting, and the direct influence of the biological environment. Genes ("nature") and the conditions of life ("nurture")—in the euphonious opposition from Shakespeare's *The Tempest*—stood as opposing one another.[15]

These "neo-Lamarckian" geneticists, on the other hand, maintained that you are crucially a product of your upbringing and circumstances. One of the most prominent, and last, of this school was a biologist named Paul Kammerer, who came to America on a lecture tour in 1923, hoping to teach the human race "to avoid acquired degenerate tendencies." His research, argued Kammerer, would permit us "to eliminate race hatred."[16] A noble thought, to be sure, but hardly derivable from the mating habits of toads, which is what he studied. Kammerer committed suicide a few months after the revelation that his prize toad specimen had been injected with India ink to emphasize the features that were supposed to have been produced by the inheritance of acquired characteristics.[17]

The hereditarian scientific ideology reached its zenith twice in the twentieth century—first, with the rhetoric of the eugenics movement in the 1920s, and second, with the rhetoric of the Human Genome Project in the early 1990s. In the 1920s, genetics provided a rationalization to sterilize the poor and restrict the immigration of Italians and Jews into the United States. A popular 1925 college genetics textbook warned students of "a great many people who are always on the border line of self-supporting existence and whose contribution to society is so small that the elimination of their stock would be beneficial."[18] Not by coincidence, in the 1990s, political conservatives jumped on the "geno-hype" being generated by the molecular biologists promoting the Human Genome Project, and the result was the infamous best seller *The Bell Curve*, which reiterated old arguments about imaginary racial differences in intelligence being at the root of social inequality.

Epigenetics can thus be seen as the modern scientific reaction against the hereditarian thought that rode in on the rhetoric of the Human Genome Project, which was busily justifying itself with claims like "we now know, in large measure, our fate is in our genes."[19] It provides an explanation in cellular Mendelian genetics for the influence of the environment upon the body, and as well for the manner in which we are actually more than our own DNA sequences, and more than our ancestors' DNA sequences.

THE EXPLOITIVE SYSTEM

The third evolutionary system once again highlights the non-passivity of the organism. It is the relationship between organisms and their surroundings. Animals live where they are familiar and safe. Classically, ecologists recognized the fit between an organism and its environment, and saw the environmental niche as a static "given" to which the organism's ancestors had gradually become adapted. Subsequent generations of scholars, however, came to appreciate that the environment is itself dynamic and reactive, because the organism doesn't simply "occupy" a niche, but interacts with its environment and transforms it.[20] The organism is not an automatic outgrowth of its genotype, but a reactive agent; and the environment is neither stable nor independent of the organism. The descendants thus have to coadapt in harmony with the new environments created by their own ancestors. The most important such transformation was probably engendered by the cyanobacteria hundreds of millions of years ago, photosynthesizing on an earth without atmospheric oxygen. By transforming the atmosphere, they made it possible for multicellular animal life to evolve.

In the case of human evolution, these generalizations reach their apotheosis. The ecological focus of human evolution involves the extent to which our ancestors were not embedded as "animals" in a local "environment," but rather, brought environments with them, created familiar environments in unfamiliar places, and proceeded to transform wherever they were into images of what they wanted it to be.

Even with brains half the size of our own, our ancestors were looking at the world in a wholly new way, asking what they could do with the things around them. Not only did they transform rocks into tools, but the rocks eventually reciprocally transformed their hands into better tool-using appendages. Chimpanzees don't do much with tools for two reasons: they have small, weak brains and small, weak thumbs. Using their hands to either hang from or to support their weight when on the ground, apes have long fingers and short thumbs. Probably the only test of strength in which you could beat a chimpanzee is in the children's game of thumb wrestling. In other words, tools coevolved with manual dexterity.[21] The net effect was the evolution of a creature who had not only the desire, but the ability, to see the world as composed of ingredients or raw materials to make things out of.

One interesting consequence of banging rocks together, or rubbing things vigorously, is that sometimes they get warm or throw off sparks. If you choose the right materials, and work at it carefully for a few hundred thousand years, you can become very adept at producing fire when you need it. And the most obvious value of fire is that it allows you to take your environment with you wherever you go. It's warmth and protection from predators, at the very least. It's a light in the dark. It also permits the transformation of inedible or indigestible foods into edible and more digestible foods.[22] Between the ability to control fire and the ability to skin and work animal hides with their sharp stones, our hominid ancestors could construct environments for themselves in places that would have uninhabitable for their own ape ancestors.

Along with tools and fire, animal hides could be used to make a second skin (i.e., clothing), as well as to help construct a shelter from the elements (i.e., early dwellings). We don't know when this began, but our ancestors were probably doing it by a few hundred thousand years ago.

The fourth mode by which early humans constructed niches involved importing raw materials from far away, so that they had these objects at their disposal where the objects did not occur naturally. This involved networks of exchanges and reciprocal obligations with other human groups in different areas—in a word, trade.[23] Unlike the networks imagined by modern economists, based on modern markets in which every participant tries to maximize gain and get the most for the least, the networks of early humans probably involved cooperation and ritualized exchange, based instead on ethnographic inference.[24] Personal gain at someone else's expense was probably less of a motivation than mutual aid,[25] at very least since these partners would probably be standing in some sort of permanent relationship with one another, linked by bonds of kinship and an understanding of their future expectations from one another.

Finally, early people developed relationships with other animal species that once again created environments previously unknown. Long before these species were maintained and selectively bred (only a few thousand years ago), they probably coexisted with people symbiotically, in ways that benefited both parties. We can only imagine what those ways might have been, but the fact that early humans were drilling holes in mammalian teeth, and sometimes leaving their dead with animal parts,[26] suggests that they theorized their coexistence with other species. The earliest carvings we know of, from about 40,000 years ago, are half human, half lion—which suggests that early people thought about their relationships with animals in complex and symbolic ways. The fact that early people utilized shells and rocks and plants, but generally depicted only other mammals, likewise attests to the idea that they thought a lot about, and interacted intimately with, other mammalian species long before penning them up and breeding them.

The most significant aspect of this mode of niche construction came about with the domestication of plants and animals, and the decision to begin producing food. This took place in different parts of the Old World, with different kinds of species, between about 12,000 and 4,000 years before the present. This permitted human societies to control the means of their own subsistence and to store and redistribute the surpluses, although it led immediately to nutritional imbalances, and eventually to gross disparities in wealth and status. One could reasonably argue that much of the modern world is a direct social and economic consequence of the choice that those people made, a few thousand years ago, to begin messing around with the gene pools of their familiar animal and plant species. (This is quite different from modern issues surrounding genetically modified foods, however, since Monsanto isn't exactly "people," and the question of the scope, goals, and consequences of such modification today are not comparable to those of several millennia ago.)

THE CULTURAL SYSTEM

This evolutionary system (omitted by Waddington) involves learned behaviors, which exist in other species, but which are elaborated and embellished in human evolution by the development of symbolic thought, essentially creating environments and adaptations out of the imagination. To the extent that these imaginings may be realized, people live very different kinds of ecological lives than do our close relatives, the apes. At the very least, culture transforms what are ecological relationships in other species into economic relationships in humans. Anthropologist Clyde Kluckhohn noted (in quaintly sexist terms) that "culture can be regarded as that part of his environment that is the creation of man."[27]

What permits this organically lies in the product of our brain, that is to say, our mind. The human mind seems to be uniquely capable of four processes, which shape the way we interact with our world, and essentially create it.[28] The first is that we think hierarchically, not in terms of all the world's elements being equivalently elemental, but in terms of "this is a kind of that." That's the basis of classifying, which we do to everything from relatives to colors to plants. Often there are many possible dimensions by which to classify: for example, we could focus on the use of a chair and classify it along with a bed as "furniture," or on the quadrupedal structure of a chair and classify it along with a deer as "something with four legs," or on the composition of the chair and classify it along with a tree as "made of wood." The choice we make depends on the purpose of the classification, and sometimes on simply arbitrary decisions that our ancestors made for us. Is a dolphin a kind of fish on account of where it lives and how it moves, or a kind of mammal on account of its physiology and evolutionary history? We'll call it a kind of mammal because we will privilege the second set of criteria over the first, but certainly the first set makes a certain degree of sense too.

The second way we think is symbolically, making arbitrary associations between things that have no intrinsic connection to one another. The most basic example of this is pointing, which humans are doing in their first year, but chimps just don't do. They can be intensively trained to do it a little, rather like they can be trained to walk and to smoke cigarettes while riding bicycles, but pointing is just not a chimpanzee thing. It is simply an imaginary connection between the tip of the index finger and an object out there, but it exists only in the mind of the pointer and of someone with a similarly built brain.[29]

The third way we think is creatively, taking information from different domains and putting them together in new ways. Probably the most basic way of doing this is by the use of simile. a mountain may be like a molehill, a cloud may be like the silhouette of a face, a lion may be like a brave, strong friend. These juxtapositions or combinations may have been thought of before or they may be brand-new, but this manner of thought opens up essentially an infinitely expandable array of possibilities. Anything can in principle be associated with anything else, if you just think about it the right way.

And finally, we think abstractly. That is to say, we conceive of things that don't exist or will never exist or have never existed—and we can treat them as if they were just as real as things that do exist or did exist or will exist. Burying the dead, for example, was being carried out by prehistoric peoples 100,000 years ago, despite being a waste of time and protein. The reason has something to do with love or respect or memory—but it involves a conception of the idealized past or the imagined future, not the lifeless present.

Human thought, however, is only the merest aspect of being human—for it is organic and internal. The more significant part for our evolution is what it allows us to do among ourselves, the "superorganic" aspects of human existence, which involve the relations among people formed by our communication system, quite unique in the history of life.

What language does for us is not simply to allow us to have abstract thoughts, but it compels us to share them, and thus opens up a social universe of imagining, planning, and cooperating. This, in turn, permits us to construct our own niches—but not simply in relation to our physical survival and comfort. We create historical and social environments as well, which we were born into and we have to adapt to. Language is the most fundamental of these environments, both a function of our organic, cognitive processes, and yet also a construction of history and culture.

The primary effect of language is that it allows us to know what is going on in someone else's mind—because, unlike other species, they can tell us. This forms the basis for the coordinated activity that characterizes human behavior. Along with the ability to tell someone what you are thinking comes the ability to reinforce that information with highly developed facial musculature, eyebrows, and eye whites, which readily combine to communicate a range of gross feelings, such as happiness, rage, disgust, surprise, boredom, and sadness, as well as more subtle things, like bliss, irony, and romance. It also comes with the ability to deceive others into misreading your intentions, for your own benefit, which in turn has raised the possibility in the minds of some scientists that we evolved not so much to be cooperators, but rather to be schmucks, for our intelligence is there by virtue of having facilitated the development of deceit in our ancestors.[30] The fact, however, that we *can* do something does not mean that we evolved *to* do it, a well-known fallacy known as adaptationism. The fact that we can do cartwheels does not mean we evolved to do cartwheels; it only means that the properties that we did evolve also permit that activity. Seeing humans as naturally prosocial or antisocial simply recapitulates an old philosophical argument—for example, Thomas Hobbes in the mid-seventeenth century seeing people primordially as solitary and competitive, and Giambattista Vico in the early eighteenth century seeing people as primordially cooperative and social.[31] Our evolutionary history involves the propensities to be both cooperative and manipulative, but the cooperative, prosocial features seem to be the ones that got us where we are in the history of life.

What we do not know is whether language (as vocal symbolism) emerged from primordial ape vocalizations that became symbolic, or from primordial symbolic acts that became vocal. Ape vocalizations are not conversational (that is to say, alternating, so that one ape goes "oo-oo-oo" and then gives another ape a turn). They appear, rather, to be contagious, like laughter; that is, one ape goes "oo-oo-oo," and the others join in. Further, we humans control our breathing so that we vocalize almost exclusively while we exhale. That's not true for the chimp vocalizations. The inference, then, is that ape vocalizations are homologous to laughter rather than to speech, which in turn suggests that ape vocalizations are not the evolutionary source of human language.[32] Instead, it seems more likely that human language is the result of symbolic acts—like pointing, gesturing, and dancing—whose cognitive associations became transferred and eventually co-opted by the vocal apparatus.

One such symbolic act involves bodily decoration, a distinctly human feature. Clothing is not just utilitarian, but communicative; and early humans were probably decorating themselves in other ways—with pigments and jewelry—at least as soon as they began dressing. Indeed, cutting and tending the hair on our head must have coevolved with the technology to do so, and again is far more functional symbolically than biologically. The earliest depictions of the human form, the Venus figurines from about 25,000 years ago, show the hair being carefully tended, back in the Stone Age. This is classic symbolic anthropology: we associate short hair with convicts, soldiers, and businessmen; and long hair with hippies, geniuses, and artists. The connection is subtle but wide ranging, and it seems to be about being close to the nexus of social power, either having it imposed on you, or wielding it yourself. Long hair is symbolically associated with being less controllable. The point is that hair communicates social information about its bearer.[33] It requires constant tending, and it's uniquely human; apes don't have to worry about it. But humans have to, because if they don't, it overgrows their sensory apparatus, which would be patently maladaptive. Head hair had to coevolve with the ability and interest in taking care of it. And what that suggests is that we are dealing with minds that are familiar; they are like our own in some fundamental way, making statements about who we are through our personal grooming habits. This, once again, emphasizes the fact that internal human mental processes are creating external meanings and relationships that connect humans invisibly and symbolically to one another. What is unusual from the standpoint of evolution is that those external, or extrasomatic, connections can outlive the bodies of their bearers, which is in large measure the distinguishing feature of human culture.[34]

Consider two fundamental human attributes: language and kinship. A human is born into both. You probably didn't choose to learn English, and you definitely did not choose to be a son or daughter, brother or sister, grandchild, nephew or niece. Those slots existed before you appeared, and you learned how to occupy them; and English existed before you appeared, and you learned how to speak it. Moreover, although you learned English, you didn't learn all of English. Nobody knows all of English; it's larger than any single person's scope of knowledge, and always has been. Likewise, nobody knows all of kinship; in most cultures, the knowledge of how to be a son is different from the knowledge of how to be a daughter, for example; the people who know what to do when a woman is delivering a baby may not know how to trade properly with neighboring peoples or how to make an arrowhead. Consequently, it is not quite right to identify culture as the knowledge that an individual possesses, as biologists and psychologists sometimes do, for no individual in any culture possesses all the knowledge of that culture. Culture, in other words, is bigger than the individuals who possess its knowledge. That doesn't mean that it can't be directed or influenced; just that it can't be possessed, only sampled.

The most directly observable way that humans adapt is technologically, and technological evolution has autocatalytic properties that are quite distinct from the organic properties of the natural world. This arises from the fact that the same technology used for survival and food procurement may be useful in aggression and defense. If you don't have the most up-to-date and efficient militia or defenses, your neighbors are likely to. And even if they decide not to try and annex you with their technological superiority, they will be just a bit more likely to be able to ward off an attack when your common enemy sweeps down from the north. We now live in an age in which technology is not just a military commodity but forms the basis of our entire economy. And we have arrived at a familiar situation, in which you expect your children's technological world to be unfamiliar to you. And yet, only few generations ago, most people in the world anticipated that their children's lives would be pretty much the same as their own.

As we noted in chapter 2, when viewing technology, the long lens of history sees progress and acceleration. Other aspects of culture invariably change, often in reaction to technology, but not necessarily toward objective improvement. Kinship changes (for example, with the large number of single working parents, and the introduction of the kin term "baby daddy"), and language changes (with "twerking" and "selfies") , but it's not clear whether those constitute improvement, degradation, or some kind of random motion.

THE NATURAL SELECTIVE SYSTEM

The variations produced by mutation may ultimately be preserved or perpetuated in future generations if they are favorable, or they may be rejected or destroyed if they are injurious, as Darwin recognized. But variations in what? Darwin clearly meant body parts, but subsequent generations of geneticists transferred Darwin's meaning to genes—by simply equating a species with a gene pool, a body with a genome, and particular attributes of bodies with genes themselves. Thus, the geneticist Theodosius Dobzhansky could reduce evolution to "a change in the genetic composition of a population" or "a change in gene frequency through time." Natural selection would simply be the disproportional representation of one or the other genetic variants in future generations.

By the 1980s, a bifurcation had occurred within the study of natural selection. The behaviorists or ethologists were adopting the reductive definition and extending it even more broadly—now talking about competition among alleles, and "the selfish gene." On the other hand, mainstream evolutionary biologists were rejecting the reductive definition altogether, for its failure to grapple with the interaction among genes in producing phenotypes, a failure that Ernst Mayr called "beanbag genetics." The reductive approach failed to problematize the body, which was implicitly simply the sum of its genes; and failed to conceptualize variation and competition among elements at different levels of a natural hierarchy—between organisms or populations or species.[35] After all, the reductive definition addressed simply the transformation of a lineage through time, and not the multiplication of lineages.

The "change in gene frequencies in a population" was evolution all right, but it constituted evolution's minor features; evolutionary biologists like George Gaylord Simpson were interested in its major features.[36] No one doubted—as Darwin took great pains to demonstrate—that the differences one observed within populations, and the processes that produced them, were effectively the same as, but smaller in scale than, those that one observed between species. Nevertheless, it was difficult to see how a well-studied microevolutionary genetic phenomenon—like the spread of the allele for sickle-cell anemia in Africa—

actually afforded an adequate description of, say, bipedalism, assuming one could just wait and observe for hundreds of thousands of years.

The problem lay in the facile translation between genetic constitution and body, or between genotype and phenotype. Fruit-fly genetics and human medical genetics had converged on a system of discovering and naming genes, which focused on their major pathological effects. Consequently, geneticists had learned rather little about how genes build a normal, working body, and rather much about how to screw up that process. There are, after all, many more ways to make a bad soufflé than there are to make a good one. Even today, in the wake of the Human Genome Project, we know that it takes two genomes to build a person, and almost nothing about why one or three won't cut it.[37]

Natural selection, then, involves the often passive competition between biological forms, for representation in future generations. Such competition requires two attributes: reproducing, or copying; and interacting in some way with an external world that promotes or inhibits that replicative process. We find those properties in three kinds of biological forms: cells, organisms, and species. Cells generally reproduce mitotically and interact physiologically; organisms generally replicate sexually and interact socially; species generally replicate geographically and interact ecologically.

The cells in your body are programmed for division (mitosis), harmonious interaction with other cells, and death (apoptosis). Cells that cheat, by replicating uncontrollably, manage to outbreed the other cells in the short run, but kill the organism of which they are a part. Hereditary cancer consequently is a disease primarily of the middle-aged and elderly, who have finished reproducing—for cancers that strike young people essentially doom themselves. The life cycle of the organism thus places constraints upon the behavior of its cells.

In parallel, the population can place constraints on what organisms can do. In a classic argument, animals can't reduce their breeding for the good of the group, since anyone who doesn't do it ("cheaters") will quickly outbreed the rest. (Since breeding represents evolutionary fitness in the most literal sense, this is the most quintessentially altruistic act in biology, from which all others are simply mathematical deviations.) The only way that lowering your own fitness for the good of the group could happen is if the organisms had foresight (which of course they don't) or coercive mechanisms by which to discourage cheaters (which they don't either). On the other hand, you don't have to think too hard to come up with one species that has both foresight and coercive institutions, so the constraint that "things can't evolve for the good of the group" does not carry weight in *Homo sapiens.* As the evolutionary geneticist Francisco Ayala put it,

> The fitness advantage of selfish over altruistic behavior does not necessarily apply to humans, because humans can *understand* the benefits of altruistic behavior (it benefits the group but indirectly it benefits them as well) and thus adopt altruism and protect it, by laws or otherwise, against selfish behavior that harms the social group.[38]

The differential replication of variants due to the constraints of their setting can thus take place at different levels of a natural hierarchy, and can impact the patterns discernible at other levels. Rates of speciation and extinction of populations, for example, may affect what appear to be the simple proportions of alleles or organisms in a species. More significant, however, is that we formally distinguish between natural selection, as a consistent and non-random bias across generations that shapes the gene pool to fit its circumstances, and genetic drift, as a one-off random blow or tweak to the gene pool. Consequently, studies that examine a snapshot of behaviors or alleles at a single time, and find them to be more-or-less in tune with a hypothesis, and conclude that this is evidence of selection at work, are not really finding evidence of selection, because its most salient point is that multigenerational consistency. We know that the genome can produce non-adaptation and maladaptation, and that bodies can make do with a lot of physical noise, while still maintaining a passable level of functionality; that is the crucial distinction between Herbert Spencer's "survival of the fittest" and the Darwinian survival of the fit.

CHAPTER FIVE

How Our Ancestors Transgressed the Boundaries of Apehood

It has long been known that humans resemble monkeys in interesting ways, but nineteenth-century Europeans innovatively began to interpret that resemblance as a trail of common descent, literally a family resemblance. There are two groups of animals living in the Old World that are especially similar to our own genes and bodies. The more distant are known as monkeys, and their bodies are built for a four-legged gait, walking on branches and the ground, with their fingers extended and with a long spine, ending in a tail of variable length. The other group is known as apes, and its members are built for hanging from branches, suspending themselves. Their shoulders move differently; their hands while in the trees are like hooks, and when they come to the ground, their fingers are flexed, to varying extents. And since they spend a lot of their time hanging in a nearly vertical posture, they use their spine differently, and it is shorter and stiffer than a monkey's. By the eighteenth century, the French naturalist Count de Buffon could complain that English possessed an advantage over French in making that crucial distinction:

> The English are not reduced, as we are, to a single name for the *singes;* they have, like the Greeks, two different names, one for tailless *singes,* which they call "ape," and the other for the tailed *singes,* which they call "monkey."[1]

Our anatomy places us among the apes, as we have a similar shoulder and a short, fairly rigid spine. Our genes link us especially to those animals as well. Yet we are obviously different from the apes, in speaking, striding, and cooking, as well as in less archaeologically detectable—but possibly just as important—ways, like pointing, sweating, and following rules. It was Darwin who recognized that the best explanation of the physical similarity was as a trail of common descent (as the early philologists had appreciated about the similarities of languages from Ireland to India, a half century before *The Origin of Species*[2]).

Phylogeny and classification are different things: one is history; the other is language. One may be based on the other to greater or lesser extents, but they are different classes of facts. As we noted in chapter 1, the question of your relationship to your ancestors—Are you simply them?—is a highly biopolitical question. From the standpoint of racial ancestry, for example, your identity and your ancestry are governed by a set of cultural rules: that the categories are discrete ("racialism"); that they are deterministically associated with social, political, and economic differences ("racism"); that a little bit of lower-status ancestry overrides the higher-status ancestry ("one drop of blood"); that if you are biracial, you assume the identity of the lower-status race ("hypodescent"). Are you reducible to the properties of your ancestors ("hereditarianism"), or can you somehow be free of them? Can you be more than they were? Can you be just simply different from them?

The answer to that last question is obviously yes—after all, that is what we mean by evolution, the fact that descendants are indeed different from their ancestors. In a basic sense, then, if someone were to say, "We are apes," that statement might be construed to mean, "We have not evolved," for it fails to acknowledge the naturalistic production of difference between ancestors and descendants. In the very first book on human evolution, Thomas Huxley explained, "No one is more strongly convinced than I am of the vastness of the gulf between civilized man and the brutes; or is more certain that whether *from* them or not, he is assuredly not *of* them."[3] Huxley is explaining why you can be from the apes (ancestry), yet not be of them (identity), for you have evolved. Nearly a century later, the paleontologist George Gaylord Simpson made the same point: "It is not a fact that man is an ape, extra tricks or no.... Such statements are not only untrue but also vicious for they deliberately lead astray enquiry as to what man really is and so distort our whole comprehension of ourselves and of our proper values."[4]

Nevertheless the idea that we are an ape of some sort—that our identity, rather than just our ancestry, is that of an ape—is a common theme in the popular scientific literature. Asserted in such science best sellers as *The Naked Ape* and *The Third Chimpanzee* and *Why Evolution Is True,*[5] the assertion is a simple falsehood that miseducates the public, if we are to give any weight to the explanations and judgments of Huxley and Simpson.

The most recent assertion that "we are apes" is derived from the demonstration of our intimate similarities to the apes genetically. That, however, is simply a bias of the nature of the comparison: we don't know how to identify bipedalism, language, a chin, sweat glands, small canine teeth, morality, or any of the many and profound differences from the apes genetically. The genetic comparison reveals our ancestry more readily than our difference. As Huxley and Simpson would have argued, if you can't see our differences from the apes in a genetic comparison, why not simply look at something else?

In the present context, then, given that our ancestry is ape ancestry, it does not follow that we are apes. It could only follow if we arbitrarily gave special privilege to the data that reveal ancestry the most clearly, or if we arbitrarily reduce your identity to simply your ancestry. The "pop science" origin myth of human evolution observes the genetic intimacy of humans to apes, applies the cultural assumption that genetic relationships are the most important relationships, and concludes that our identity can be easily established from our ancestors. But as we noted in chapter 1, the fact that your ancestors may have been peasants or slaves does not make you a peasant or slave. We find the cultural idea of reducing identity to ancestry to be morally repugnant. The reason is simple, that we are different from our ancestors, and our identity is established dialectically, recognizing that we are simultaneously both composed of their DNA and yet different from them.

The genetic intimacy on which the argument that "we are apes" is based was actually known in the early part of the twentieth century. The phylogenetic distance of the Asian orangutan from the African cluster of human-chimpanzee-gorilla was explicitly understood and presented to first-year college students in Earnest Hooton's classic text, *Up from the Ape* (1946). When it was rediscovered in the 1960s, it encountered a more favorable cultural climate, in the age of molecular biology and genomics.[6] To privilege genetic relationships over other kinds of relationships, as a simple reflex, was a consequence of the "geno-hype" that accompanied the Human Genome Project toward the end of the twentieth century. It is *not* the case that DNA comparisons encapsulate species comparisons; if it were, then the fact that our DNA is statistically constrained to match the DNA bases of asparagus at least 25 percent of the time (since there are only four bases in DNA, after all) would imply that we must see ourselves as one-quarter asparagus. Anyone who tells you such a thing is either messing with you or deranged; our DNA simply does not readily translate into a comprehensible identity for us.[7]

Moreover, to decide that we are simply reducible to our ape ancestors of 8 million years ago, even though our more recent ancestors evolved the abilities to walk and talk, hardly does credit to our fish ancestors of 400 million years ago. Why are we not fish, even though our ancestors evolved the ability to breathe air, and four limbs to support their body weight on land? We fit within the category "fish" phylogenetically, just as we fit within the category "apes"—albeit far more remotely in our ancestry. We can certainly learn something from the recognition of our ancestry, ape or fish,[8] but that is quite different from saying this is what we are.

If we are not apes, then what are we? We are ex-apes, just as we are ex-fish. Obviously, we are more similar to apes than to anything else. We are both similar to them and yet distinct from them. To emphasize the similarity to apes would lead to a classification proposed by geneticists, who would make chimpanzees another species within our genus, *Homo*.[9] To emphasize the divergence would lead to the classification of early anatomists, who separated us from all the other primates at the level of the Suborder, as "two-handed ones" or Bimana.[10] Our compromise, seeing humans and apes as parts of the same Superfamily (called Hominoidea, or hominoids, meaning "rather like humans"), comes from the 1945 classification of mammals by the paleontologist George

Gaylord Simpson. A similar compromise juxtaposes the large-bodied apes (orangutan, chimpanzee, and gorilla as Family Pongidae, or "pongids") to humans and their bipedal ancestors (Family Hominidae, or "hominids," meaning "even more like humans").[11]

In the last decade or so, as the spirit of intellectual compromise has receded in the face of genomics, some scholars have reduced the difference between apes and humans to a lower level, if not quite so low as the geneticists who want to separate us from chimps at the species level. This would break up the great apes and separate us from them below the Superfamily, below the Family, and even below the Subfamily, instead separating us at an obscure level, the Tribe. Here, humans and their bipedal relatives would be called the Tribe Hominini, or "hominins," meaning "incredibly similar to humans."[12]

Calling humans and their fossil relatives "hominins," though, is thus not based upon any new discoveries, but rather upon the application of the contestable cultural assumption that genetic similarities are more important than cognitive, social, or physical differences. This affords a window on the bio-cultural nature of anthropological systematics, in which the number of species identifiable within the genus *Homo* may be as low as two (*erectus* and *sapiens*) or as high as fourteen (*antecessor, georgicus, pekinensis, floresiensis, neanderthalensis, gautengensis, habilis, ergaster, rhodesiensis, cepranensis, rudolfensis, helmei, erectus,* and *sapiens,* not to mention Denisovans[13]). We sometimes call scholars who group many fossils into a few species "lumpers," and scholars who group a few fossils into lots of species "splitters." But this is not capricious (as the distinction between "lumpers" and "splitters" tends to imply); rather, it is strategic, for there are professional payoffs for "splitting." After all, more species means more key specimens, and more key specimens means more important people control-

TABLE I

Contrasting classifications of living humans and great apes

Family Pongidae	Family Pongidae
Genus *Pongo*	Genus *Pongo*
Genus *Pan*	Family Hominidae
Genus *Gorilla*	Subfamily Homininae
Family Hominidae ("hominids")	Genus *Pan*
Genus *Homo*	Genus *Gorilla*
	Tribe Hominini ("hominins")
	Genus *Homo*

On the left, a classification that privileges the adaptive specializations of the human lineage, and sets off humans from the other three genera. Here, our species and its fossil relatives are called "hominids." On the right, a classification that privileges genetic relationships and proximity of descent, and sets off orangutans from the other three genera. Here, our species and its fossil relatives are called "hominins."

ling them. And "splitting" enables Spain, Georgia, China, Indonesia, South Africa, Kenya, Zambia, and Italy each to have their own species, and thus each be a key player in the unfolding scientific narrative of human origins.

Species here are not "natural" units, but "natural/cultural" units. They are not built up from facts of nature, but are made as well from the concerns and interests of the classifier, who works partly according to the cultural mind-set and issues of the age. One major scientific concern today is conservation. Most primate species are threatened in the wild. Legislation written to protect them has tended to focus on species. It may be in corporate interests, then, to define the range of a species very widely, so that they can cut down the forest over here, but there will still be some members of the species left over there. And to restore the spirit of the law, we declare that the primates over here are a different species from the one over there, and they are both endangered. That's why textbooks twenty-five years ago said there were about 170 species of primates, but textbooks today say there are over 400. We haven't discovered many new ones, and they aren't speciating like mad. But they are multiplying. Most of the "speciation" is really the recognition that two groups of animals that had previously been considered subspecies, races, varieties, or local populations ought now to be considered as separate species.[14] We universally accept that conservation is the most important issue facing both primates and primatologists. After all, without primates there can be no primatology. It is simply far more important to preserve them than to tally them up. So the primates win, the environment wins, and all we have had to do is subtly reconceptualize a species from a unit of evolution to a unit of conservation. This is known as "taxonomic inflation" and is not limited to primate taxonomy. To understand it, you have to realize that a species is not a unit of nature, but a unit of nature/culture or bio-culture. You can certainly argue about what you think a species is or ought to be, but eventually you run into the fact that it is quite simply more important to save the primates than it is to count them—except, perhaps, to some kind of heartless pedant or corporate shill.

The point is that fossil hominid species are products of nature/culture, and so are the living primate species. It's not that there is no reality; it's just that the nature of reality is different from what you may have thought it was.

These are not scientific facts whose true qualities could be discerned by a truly objective observer, someone who could manage to free themselves of the confounding effects of culture, and see the world clearly. Thomas Huxley suggested pretending that you're from Saturn. Jared Diamond, many years later, suggested pretending that you're from Mars. This is, of course, no science argument at all, but a science fiction argument, built to reinforce the unexamined arrogance of ethnocentric scientific judgments. Those scholars had no better idea about how extraterrestrials would think than you or I do. Indeed, they may have had less of an idea, since they seem to underestimate the diversity of ways and criteria that terrestrial human societies use to classify things.

More interesting, however, is the implicit assumption about the relations between the objective world of nature and the subjective world of culture; it presumes that culture is like the icing on a cake, which needs to be scraped off to reveal nature underneath it. But what if, instead, culture were not like the icing on the cake, but like the eggs in the cake? What if it is impossible to be a scientist outside of culture, external to its assumptions, metaphors, prejudices, and priorities? Then perhaps the best you can do is to try to be as self-analytic as possible, identify the biases of your predecessors, and try to transcend your own.

This is a much more real situation in the study of human evolution, because human evolution is our origin narrative, and such narratives universally have cultural salience. Trying to navigate through the primates in his monograph on mammalian classification, George Gaylord Simpson sighed in print,

> Perhaps it would be better for the zoological taxonomist to set apart the family Hominidae and to exclude its nomenclature and classification from his studies.[15]

HUMAN ANCESTRY

Let us proceed with the assumption that the specific details (such as "*Homo ergaster*") tend to be trivial and often short-lived. The bigger picture (at the genus level) is clearer, because the genera represent organisms with different basic adaptations, and which consequently approach their own survival in different ways, which can be identifiable in the paleontological or archaeological record.

Thus, we generally recognize our lineage as beginning with a bipedal adaptation, and ascribed to the genus *Australopithecus*. This genus has been regarded, since being first described in 1925, as a "missing link" because of its combination of human and simian features. These, most generally, are a brain like an ape's, yet teeth like a human and the hallmarks of the human bipedal habit. *Australopithecus* now encompasses material from South and East Africa, ranging from about 4.5 to about 2 million years ago, with the famous fossil "Lucy" falling right in the middle of that range. While earlier material is far more ambiguously bipedal, we find two suites of human-like features in *Australopithecus:* first, a change in the teeth, from an emphasis on the front teeth (as in apes) to the back teeth (as in humans); and second, a change in the manner of locomotion, from the suspensory and quadrupedal gaits of apes to the obligate bipedalism of humans. This is detectable all through the body, from the base of the skull to the heel of the foot. The brain of *Australopithecus,* however, is more like an ape's—only about one-third the size of ours.

In the case of locomotion, moving the head and center of gravity from in front of the pelvis to atop the pelvis, and changing the primary function of the feet from grasping structures to weight-bearing structures, created a suite of subtle, yet diagnostic criteria for distinguishing the body of an ape from that of a human ancestor. The human spine is more curved; the hands are relieved of weight bearing; the pelvis, hip, and knee support the body's weight, rather than trailing after it; the foot is more stable and less flexible, and the big toe has adjusted for weight bearing rather than for grasping. Even the human skull and neck differ anatomically from the ape's by virtue of sitting atop the body, rather than ahead of it.[16]

Yet even for such a fundamental feature as bipedality, we know far more about *how* it evolved than about *why* it evolved.[17] We can certainly see the differences it wrought upon ancestral ape anatomy; it was clearly very important. And from the anatomical comparisons, we can tell you how that evolution occurred—what parts of the body changed, and how they changed. And that's boring, because it's anatomy. What we can't tell you is *why* it happened. That is history, that is origin myth, that is interesting. On the other hand, if a chimpanzee is chasing you to rip your face off, it is going to catch you. You can't outrun it, because our mode of locomotion makes us a lot slower than an ape.

Presumably being bipedal was good for something, and it had to be good enough to overcome the disadvantage of slowing us down. But we do not know, and quite possibly never will know, because it may be unknowable, exactly what bipedalism was good for. The fact that apes sometimes stand erect when threatening one another, the fact that humans can run longer distances than apes, the fact that having your eyes higher off the ground allows you to see farther—and many others—have been suggested as scenarios for the evolution of bipedalism.[18] That is to say, it must have been good for something. What these propositions all share is the property of futility. If there was an advantage to bipedality, we can't tell what it was, from our vantage point of 5 or 6 million years later. Consequently we have to side with Isaac Newton, who was challenged on the question of where gravity came from, given that he seemed to have figured out how it worked. "I make no hypotheses," said Newton; and that should be our guide. We have to bracket the question "Why did we become bipedal?" and set it off from more empirically based scientific discourse on the subject.

We will always be caught in Newton's trap, however. Once you have figured out how gravity works, *why it is there* becomes a far more interesting question, albeit an unscientific one. It is the narrative, mythic component of the story; the one far less circumscribed by data and rigorous analysis. Likewise, *why we are bipedal* is more interesting, but less scientific, than how we got that way. Nevertheless, the very use of bipedalism as an evolutionary marker conceals a shorthand. After all, as we will see in chapter 6, chimpanzees and gorillas can walk bipedally when they choose to. When we talk of the human condition, we are actually talking about the loss of that choice.

The descendants of *Australopithecus* retained the bipedality and the small front teeth, and evolved in two directions. One, *Paranthropus,* will rely on the dental adaptation, and will take that adaptation even further, with tiny front teeth and enlarged back teeth and heavy chewing muscles for intense crushing and grinding. The other, *Homo,* sharpens the hand-eye coordination, increasingly relying on the products of mental and physical labor for survival. The inference of ancestry from *Australopithecus* is based on the anatomical and temporal continuity that we can identify in the fossil record.[19]

Homo, by about 1.5 million years ago, has tweaked bipedalism so that the genus possesses our own body proportions, rather than the apishly long arms and short legs of the earlier bipeds. Over its duration, we see a two- or threefold expansion of the skull, and a concomitant increasing sophistication of stone tool types.[20] This manner of interacting with the environment, by transforming it and recreating it technologically, is successful enough, even in its rudiments, that *Homo* settles as well in Asia, and later, in Europe—a range far more extensive than that of *Australopithecus* or *Paranthropus*. The fact that this adaptation is based on skills that must be learned, and can be adequately performed in many different ways, suggests that we are dealing with the elaboration of a less accessible adaptation—namely, culture—in which there emerge group-specific ways of doing things.

But let us not abandon locomotion so fast. After all, a human baby isn't born doing it properly, as, say, an elephant or dolphin baby is. Primate babies often cling to their mother's fur for a period of time before they even attempt to move around by themselves. But two years before you can actually move properly? That's a lot to ask of a human child—and, as long as there is a model around to observe, they come through nearly every time, eventually running and walking. Indeed, like our communication system, we are programmed to learn to locomote.

The last human physical features to emerge are our foreheads and chins, detectable by 150,000 years ago, in East Africa. As we will see in chapter 6, the evolution of our species increasingly shifts from the biological to the bio-cultural, and understanding biological evolution helps us understand the human condition less and less. Say what you want about the stories that we call Greek myths, but at least those pagans had an explanation for where fire, for example, came from. It came from Prometheus, as noted in chapter 2, and he paid dearly for it. But that's more than the Bible says. The Bible doesn't even try to explain the origin of fire; it's just there. Nobody has to invent it or discover it or learn to control it.[21] But hearths dating back to 300,000 years tell us that our ancestors did learn to control it.

Our ancestors were coloring things by 100,000 years ago (although we don't know exactly what they were coloring), carving images by 40,000 years ago, and drawing on cave walls by 35,000 years ago. By about 10,000 years ago some humans were living in communities and relying on farming and herding, and controlling their own subsistence. This had many side effects, however, especially of creating wealth, and distributing it (and the power it buys) unevenly among different people. Consequently, although there are still fluctuations accruing to our gene pools, our basic interactions with the external world have shifted over the course of the evolution of our species from principally biological adaptation, like other animals, to principally cultural. This was catalyzed by the emergence of a new way of communicating, about whose origins we have little direct information. This symbolic mode of communication, or language, is based on learning the meaningful associations and divisions among sounds, things, and ideas, which create the new interactions among people, the social conditions of life.

HEADS, WE WIN

The relationship between the head and the mind is a subtle one, and it has led generations of scientists into difficult straits. The brain is inside the head. Aside from Aristotle and his most devout followers (who thought that the brain's primary function was to cool the body), nearly all ancient and modern European scholars have understood the brain's primary function to be to produce thoughts. Yet different people have different thoughts— some bad, some good. And some people have mental gifts—for mathematics, for art, for socializing. Is it because they have different kinds of brains? Is it because they have different kinds of heads?

Perhaps we should look to science to find out.

In the first half of the nineteenth century, phrenology, developed by medical anatomists, was one of the most popular applied sciences.[22] It answered the question "Why do people have such different personalities?" by recourse to medical anatomy. The logic, primitive if comprehensible, was that people have different personalities because they have different brains; the brain is composed of various modules for music, love, fidelity, and the like, and since the skull encloses the brain, we can read one's personal talents and abilities from the overdeveloped or underdeveloped parts of their brain, which are inscribed upon the surface of the skull. Just as a home-wrapped Christmas present might contain a bulge for a part that is a bit too large for its box, so too does the skull have bulges corresponding to the overdeveloped parts of the brain governing particular personality attributes. All we need to do, then, is to feel the bumps on your skull, and we can tell you about your latent abilities.

By the latter part of the nineteenth century, this was generally looked upon scornfully by the mainstream anatomical community, which had its own crude logical practice. Just as a large pancreas secretes more insulin, it stands to reason that a large brain secretes more thoughts. Thus, people with large brains are more intellectually gifted than people with smaller brains.[23] One of the strongest early advocates of this idea, Samuel George Morton of Philadelphia in the 1840s, was also a believer in phrenology. And yet, it was not too difficult to find small-brained geniuses and big-brained dummies.

Perhaps, then, the head's gross shape had something to do with it, in addition to the head's gross size and surface details, or perhaps instead of them. Some people (and populations) had long heads; others had short, broad heads. Standardized measurements and a pompous scientific vocabulary developed in the middle of the nineteenth century described long-heads as doli-chocephalic and broad-heads as brachycephalic. As descriptions of people, of course, they were fine, but as explanations for their histories and social conditions, they were nonsensical, even if scientifically mainstream.[24]

The early anthropologist Franz Boas began to debunk the value of head shape, for any other purpose than descriptive, by empirically contrasting the head shapes of immigrants with the heads of their children and other family members, and showing that this trait was heavily influenced by the environment.[25] On the other hand, the early physical anthropologist Aleš Hrdlička wrote with dismissive condescension about phrenology, but when given the chance to examine the brain of a recently deceased Eskimo (Inuit) from Greenland, he leapt at the opportunity. His 1901 paper, "An Eskimo Brain," was not followed by "An Eskimo Arm" or "An Eskimo Liver," so he clearly regarded the organ as one of especially great scientific interest. It is not clear, though, just what he expected to learn from it, although he quite ghoulishly con-cluded, "The marked differences ... from those of the whites ... makes a future acquisition of Eskimo brains very desirable."[26]

By the 1920s, it had become clear that culture was not to be found inside people's brains, but rather, constituted a part of the environment that imposed itself upon people's brains. This is not to say that all brains are identical, but like arms and livers, their differences are largely irrelevant to the question of why different groups of people behave as they do, or have the histo-ries that they do. In pathological cases, the structure of a brain might be interesting, but it functions pretty much the same way in all normal people, whatever language they speak, and what-ever their social background, class, diet, traditions, or values may be.

By the 1950s, the physical anthropologists had come around as well—to the recognition that measuring head size and shape had its uses, but none of them involved the question of why different groups of people think and act as they do. The eventual apprehension of this fact was doubtless a consequence of the fact that the physical anthropology of the Nazis, like their human genetics, was not all that different from its American counterpart, and had to be fundamentally reconceptualized after World War II.[27]

The head studies, however, required admitting an exception to the guiding principle of anatomy: that form follows function. The new physical anthropology,[28] christened by Sherwood Washburn in 1951, would finally follow the cultural anthropologists, and hold as axiomatic that variation in mental properties and functions is disconnected from physical variation in head form. There is a wide range of variation in normal human heads, and a wide range of variation in normal human thoughts, and they map onto one another only in the grossest or crudest of ways. You can't legitimately infer cultural difference from the observation of cranial difference, nor cultural similarity from the observation of cranial similarity. The reason is that they are epistemologically disconnected, for cultural differences are the products of history, not biology.

Thus, heads are more or less interchangeable across the great bulk of our species, and the brains inside them can do pretty much what anyone else's brain can do, except in pathological or exceedingly unusual cases. Consequently, when we encounter a modern human skull in the ethnographic, archaeological, or fossil record, we are going to assume that it housed a normal modern human brain, just like yours and mine, and consequently was capable of thinking the full range of normal modern human thoughts, just like yours and mine. That seems to be the best inference we can draw from two centuries of studying the anthropology of heads.[29]

SYMBOLIC VOCAL COMMUNICATION, OR LANGUAGE

Physical anthropologist Wilton Krogman wrote a classic article in 1951 for *Scientific American* called "The Scars of Human Evolution."[30] It explained how bipedalism, the defining trait of our lineage, compromised with our bodies. In other words, bipedalism was so central to becoming human that it outweighed the negative consequences it brought with it—like scoliosis, back pain, hemorrhoids, varicose veins, and birthing complications.

Hard as it may be to believe, the evolution of our other most basic adaptation—our symbolic mode of communication, or language—is undertheorized. Language, which is coterminous with symbolic thought—if you can think it, you can say it—was also an unusual and apparently very good evolutionary innovation. And like bipedalism, it was so good, indeed, that it created physical problems that the human body had to solve secondarily in order to make it work, and to some extent never did solve fully.

First, it expanded our heads. Symbolic communication requires a big brain, as well as an extended period of immaturity in order to learn how to do it properly.[31] It is so difficult that we hardly even appreciate how difficult it is. From the bottom up, we learn what sounds make sense. Are "s" and "sh" variants of the same sound, or different sounds? What about "l" and "r"? Or "r" and "rr"? Or the "Ch" in "Chanukah" or the "Zh" in "Zsa-Zsa"? Are they their own sounds, or some weird variants of "Hanukah" and "Cha-Cha"? If you use that sound, you're not from around here, or you at least recognize the word that contains it as not being one of our own words. What about the "sh" sound in "shibboleth"? Recognizing that sound—as opposed to hearing it as a variant of the "s" sound—might be the difference between life and death. It meant a lot to the ancient Hebrews, at least—Judges 12:6 tells a story of 42,000 Ephraimites who wished they could have distinguished between those two sounds, as they were being killed off by the Gileadites on that basis. If that sounds too remote, consider the 1937 "Parsley Massacre" in which French-speaking Haitians were killed if they failed to pronounce the Spanish-speaking Dominicans' word for "parsley" properly.[32]

We also learn how to combine those sounds, and use them to refer to objects or acts or states. We could call those combinations of sounds "lexemes," but for the sake of simplicity, let's just call them "words." We also learn how to combine those words in meaningful ways—to state, inquire, praise, predict, comfort, recall, amuse, and command, using any of the myriad grammatical forms at our disposal. And on top of all that, we learn intonation, sarcasm, and bodily gestures to go along with the rules of our sounds, their correspondences, and combinations.

In this sense, obviously, our communication is not species-specific, a unitary feature to contrast to a chimpanzee's communication, but rather is highly local and community-specific in humans. It not only identifies you as a person, but it also localizes you within the category "person," and generally to a fairly narrow chunk of time and space. The price for all of this was a brain inside a baby's skull that hardly fits through the birth canal. And the solution to that problem was to make birthing social. While an ape squats and delivers, a human almost always needs to have someone else around.[33]

Second, language reorganized our throats. To help make all of those sounds, our larynx is positioned lower down in the throat than it is in apes and babies, who cannot make those sounds. Speech also necessitates far more intricate breath control than apes are capable of.[34] The price we pay is that the passage of air into our lungs and that of food into our bellies now crisscross, which they do not in apes, which means that we can choke on our food far more readily than a chimpanzee can. The solution: don't eat so fast, and try not to breathe while you are swallowing.

Third, language worked over not only our throats and brains, but our teeth as well. Monkeys and apes often have large, sexually dimorphic canine teeth, which they use as social threats and in the occasional actual fight. Classic sexual selection theory holds that in species in which males actively compete for mates, they do so using their canine teeth. In species where there is less competition for mates, because males and female pair off, the males and females have equal-sized canine teeth, as in the more-or-less monogamous gibbons. This is often invoked as evidence that sexual selection has been reduced in the human species, which may well be true. The problem is that those gibbon canines, which are non-dimorphic, are also actually quite large. Ours are non-dimorphic, but small. Why? Quite likely because it is really hard to speak intelligibly through large, interlocking canine teeth. Ask any vampire (or better yet, an actor who has played one). The price for the reduction of the canine teeth was that our canine teeth are not going to intimidate other members of our own species, nor defend us against members of other species. Good thing we started using tools.

Further, it is also not too hard to see how language could strongly mitigate the effects of sexual selection. In most primate species, a big male with big canine teeth can physically dominate not only other males, but females as well. Bonobos circumvent this by having the females become socially and sexually bonded, so that they will gang up against an aggressive male, in the present. Humans have a different solution to the same problem: language permits a victim to name her male assailant, so her friends and relatives can punish him, in the future. A human male who acts like a chimpanzee is much more likely to have to pay for it dearly.

And finally, in addition to reshaping our brains, throats, and teeth, language also reshaped our tongue. To make the sounds we do, our tongue became more muscular, rounded, and enervated than an ape's tongue. For this the cost was quite severe. An ape dissipates heat, as many mammals do, by panting. But to use your tongue primarily for talking, your body must produce another way of dissipating heat. Our ancestors did that by loading up our skin with sweat glands, for evaporative cooling. But evaporative cooling works most efficiently with bare skin; so our body hair had to get shorter and wispier than that of an ape.

For all that we don't know about the evolution of language, however, it affords us a critical lesson in human evolution and biology—namely, that "learned" and "genetic" are not antonyms. Language must be considered both "genetically programmed" (for it is the way human beings have biologically evolved to communicate)—*and* "learned" (for its content is actively acquired over the course of childhood, and sometimes later). This means that the dichotomy of genetic versus learned is necessarily a false one, for language is both. Under the appropriate minimal stimulation (i.e., hearing people speak regularly) a normal human child learns to communicate in this species-specific way, speaking to others. A normal chimpanzee never does; it's not built to.

Moreover, speech is not simply species-specific; it is also specific to one's local group. After all, "we" are not just the creatures who speak; we are the creatures who speak in a very particular way. "We" are the people who make the "sh" sound in "shibboleth," as opposed to our neighbors, the Gileadites; "we" are the people who call a book "book," as opposed to the barbarians who call it something else, like "biblos" or "sefer"; "we" are the people who don't distinguish between the "r" sound in the Spanish words "pero" and "perro," and so they sound pretty much the same to us, even though one means "but" and the other means "dog." Language is thus not merely a new medium of communication, but also at root a medium of division, a marker of belonging.[35]

Walking and talking are the two behaviors that are most fundamentally human, and it is quite extraordinary that they rhyme. So the next time you choke, sweat, scream for an epidural, or reach for a weapon to protect yourself because you lack confidence in your teeth to protect you, reflect on the fact that our body parts are interconnected, and that language was such a good way to communicate that it screwed you up in so many other ways. There is a fifth price as well for language: having to listen to people who don't know when to shut the hell up.

CHAPTER SIX

Human Evolution as Bio-cultural Evolution

There is a considerable literature from biologists explaining the evolution of morality, except that they define morality as altruism and cooperation, which is not the way anyone who thinks about morality actually defines it. Morality is the knowledge of right from wrong, and the injunction to do what's right. What is significantly different from the biological usage is that morality involves knowledge and rule-governed behavior.[1] Do chimpanzees have it? Chimpanzees certainly don't behave randomly; they generally know what they are expected to do, and what will happen to them if they don't do it. But there is a fundamental difference between not doing something because you realize that you can't get away with it, and not doing something because it is simply wrong, and we just don't do that. The latter is morality. (The former, according to the Kantians, is prudence.)

The origin of morality is the origin of humanity.[2] As noted in chapter 2, a widely misunderstood origin myth explains it fairly clearly. Once upon a time, thought the ancient Hebrews, the first man and woman lived in a beautiful garden. They were physically human, and mentally human (that is to say, they conversed about things), but not socially human. They did not know right from wrong. They lived more or less like the other animals, naked and without rules to guide them. In fact, they only had one rule: Don't learn the rules. The rules were there in the fruit of a tree—the Tree of the Knowledge of Good and Evil. But because they were little more than talking animals in human form, they couldn't even follow the one rule they had, and eventually ate the fruit, and learned the rules, of which the first was: Get dressed; animals are naked, and you shouldn't be. Once they learned the rules, though, there was no turning back. They were cast out of their idyllic garden life, and became real people, who had to work to feed themselves, and lead lives of labor and sorrow.[3]

The story in Genesis is only trivially about the biological origin of humanity (Genesis 2); it is more significantly about the cultural origin of the human condition (Genesis 3). What makes us human is knowing right from wrong, and once you know right from wrong, you can't go back to that state of blissful ignorance. That state of ignorance is amorality, and it is only partially tolerable in those who, broadly speaking, aren't considered quite fully human: animals, children, and strangers.

So amorality is not an option, goes the story, because once Adam and Eve ate that fruit they became essentially modern humans; that is to say, they became moral creatures—as are we, their descendants. But without amorality as an option, there are still two paths: morality and immorality. When Cain kills Abel, he knows it is wrong, but he does it anyway, and tries to cover it up. That is immorality, and that is not tolerable either. What we are left with is the most fundamental aspect of human society— any human society. *You must learn good from evil, and choose good, or you aren't welcome here.* The rules concerning good and evil may vary locally, but if you don't know them or don't follow them, then you cannot be a member in good standing of society—any society, anywhere.

The Garden of Eden story is thus far more significant and universal than the creationists would have it. It is about the cultural origin of the human condition: it attempts to explain the existence of rule-governed behavior, and the necessity of adherence to those rules. Without those rules, we would be animals—and I use "animals" in the cultural sense of "subhumans," not in the biological sense of "non-photosynthesizing multicellular organisms," which of course we are. And if we do not follow the rules, we will be unwelcome here, or anywhere. That point is made repeatedly in Genesis, not just to Cain, but to Noah, the only goodie in a world of baddies; and to Lot, who barely manages to escape the baddies of Sodom and Gomorrah. At least the baddies have now become more localized, and less global, but it is still about good and evil, which Adam and Eve did not have to bother with while they were in Eden.

There are a lot of ways to interpret that story, but creationists believe it should be taken essentially at face value. And at face value, it is far more about the genesis of the human condition, than of the human species.[4]

The evolutionary biologists who model "morality" focus on the Darwinian imperatives of surviving and breeding, which all species are obliged to obey. Morality, however, actually turns those Darwinian fitness imperatives on their heads. The most fundamental moral imperatives take the fitness imperatives as given, but make them more difficult to meet.

> Given that you must eat to survive, there are some things
> that you cannot eat: other people.

> Given that you must reproduce, there are some people that
> you cannot mess around with: other family members.

If maximizing your survival and breeding were really the issue, we wouldn't be crossing things off the list of available foods and partners. Morality is fundamentally rules, rules are fundamentally taboos, and the two most fundamental taboos are against cannibalism and incest. The rules are so basic, in fact, that in most cultures to break them is almost literally unthinkable. Of all the food taboos in the Bible (you can't eat pigs, rabbits, camels, lobsters ...), people aren't even mentioned. It's not that people are kosher; it's that eating human flesh is so absurd that it is actually off the Mosaic radar. The Bible talks about it as the final act of desperate, godless people—for example, in Leviticus 26:

> But if ... you disobey me, and continue hostile to me, I will continue hostile to you in fury; I in turn will punish you myself sevenfold for your sins. You shall eat the flesh of your sons, and you shall eat the flesh of your daughters. I will destroy your high places and cut down your incense altars; I will heap your carcasses on the carcasses of your idols. I will abhor you.

Incest is even more interesting. God says, "You should honor the Sabbath" (Commandment 4), but doesn't even bother to devote a commandment to "Don't fuck your sister." He eventually gets around to prohibiting that act in Leviticus 18:9, along with a proscription against dalliances with other family members.

Strangely, though, the Bible is ambiguously tolerant of incest. The Genesis patriarch Abraham actually admits to being married to his half sister, Sarah. (That won't be prohibited, though, until two books later.) His nephew, Lot, escapes from Sodom and Gomorrah with his wife and daughters, although his wife gets turned into a pillar of salt on the way out; but as soon as they reach safety, his daughters rape him. Nevertheless, despite their heinous crime, they don't spontaneously combust afterward; they just give birth to children named Moab and Ammon.

Weirdest of all is the good man, Noah, who lands the ark, lets the animals out, sees the first rainbow, and promptly gets plastered. And while passed out, he is visited by his son, Ham.

> He drank some of the wine and became drunk, and he lay uncovered in his tent. And Ham, the father of Canaan, saw the nakedness of his father, and told his two brothers outside. Then Shem and Japheth took a garment, laid it on both their shoulders, and walked backward and covered the nakedness of their father; their faces were turned away, and they did not see their father's nakedness. When Noah awoke from his wine and knew what his youngest son had done to him, he said, "Cursed be Canaan; lowest of slaves shall he be to his brothers."

What the text of Genesis 9 says is that Ham tells his brothers that he saw daddy naked, for which Noah curses Ham's son, rather than Ham himself.[5] This is hardly fair, since Canaan didn't do anything wrong, and all his father did was to tell his brothers that Noah was naked. It certainly wasn't Canaan's fault that Grampy passed out in his birthday suit, like the drunken sailor that he was.

Many centuries of reflection on this passage have led to the conclusion that it makes little sense in terms of either the magnitude of the crime committed or the (in)justice meted out. In fact, the Bible never says anywhere, even subsequently, that a boy should not see his father naked, much less that his own son will be cursed if he does. There is presumably some kind of tacit sex crime in the missing parts of the story, involving the son and the father.[6]

Both Lot and Noah are apparently victims of a form of incest—a sexual taboo involving a family member—in one case explicitly with daughters, and in the other case implicitly with a son. In both cases, though, the act is so powerful that it is probably about something else altogether—namely, politics. These are origin myths, although of a perverse sort. Back in the day, when writing was about as much of a novelty as sexting is today, there were several loosely affiliated "tribes" jockeying for position (and land) in the Near East. Three of the most prominent were the Ammonites, the Moabites, and the Canaanites. And of course, the Hebrews, who wrote the stories that have come down to us. And they all took identities from mythic ancestor/founders. The Hebrews claimed to be descended from Noah's great-grandson Eber (through one of the good sons, Shem); and thence from Jacob, who changed his name to Israel, and were thus the "children of Israel."

And who were their rivals descended from? The products of horrible sexual crimes: Noah's buggering son and Lot's twisted daughters—Canaan, Ammon, and Moab.[7]

The point is that incest is as much a political crime as a sexual crime in the Bible. It degrades the offenders into the indefinite future of their descendants, and even might suggest that those descendants are unworthy of land rights. That's powerful stuff.

Incest and cannibalism are primal and widespread taboos. To accuse someone of them is both political and dehumanizing. When the Romans wanted to demonize the Christians, they accused them of drinking baby blood, and centuries later, when the Christians wanted to dehumanize the Jews, they accused them of the same crime. In the modern imagination, vampires drink human blood, and zombies eat human brains. People just don't eat people, just as people don't have sex with family members. Sure, there are exceptions, like the Donner Party, who were starving in the snowy Sierra Nevada in 1846, or some cultures for whom human body parts are magically powerful and ritually consumed; and the incestuous dynastic pharaohs, who were living gods, after all. But mostly, if you accuse someone of either of those things, you are strongly implying that they are other-than-human. You are saying that they don't abide by the most fundamental rules that govern human societies. And you can say that in pretty much any language, for the taboo, and the implications of being accused of violating it, are quite broad.

And that is morality at its most basic. The things that you simply cannot do, for people simply don't do them, and to do them is to effectively cease to be a person. There are borderline cases, of course. Ingesting your partner's sexual fluids can be a very good thing, and not an act of cannibalism, although when an angry New Yorker shouts, "Eat me!" they don't intend it as a compliment. Likewise, marrying your first cousin still accounts for about 15 percent of marriages globally, and has actually been considered incestuous only in recent historical times.[8] It isn't prohibited in the Bible. Charles Darwin's wife, Emma Wedgwood, was his mother's brother's daughter. In fact, that marriage is legal today in California, New York, and Alabama, and illegal in Texas, Michigan, and Nevada—regardless of the fact that most modern Americans would have the same visceral reaction against cousin marriage that they have against sibling marriage.

THE ORIGIN OF THE CANNIBALISM TABOO

Why can we not dine on human flesh? In a strictly Darwinian universe, it seems to be maladaptive; after all, anything that must eat to survive would probably have a better chance of surviving if it didn't pass up that large package of protein that used to be Uncle Bob. Chimpanzees are not quite so fickle. When they kill one another's babies, they eat them. Interestingly, however, when they kill other adult chimpanzees, they usually don't eat them—although they have been known to take a few bites out of a dead grown-up here and there (usually the genitalia, as long as I have your attention). We have no idea why they make the distinction between youngsters being food and oldsters not. Humans don't make it; members of our own species, whatever their ages, are simply not a food source to a normal, ordinary human. To consume another person is to announce that you are abnormal and extraordinary or that the circumstances are.

Chimpanzees exhibit food preferences, but not taboos. Food taboos are generally part of being human, which involves imposing arbitrary symbolic divisions upon the natural world, and feeling somewhat arbitrarily that certain things are food and certain things are not food, in spite of the fact that both classes of things may be completely edible. The taboos are learned, not instinctual, because they change with the times, while still evoking diverse forms of repulsion or aversion. John the Baptist, for example, would have eaten a bowl of locusts and been appalled at the idea of eating a McRib sandwich, following the kosher laws laid down in Leviticus; but you would be hard-pressed to find a Christian or Jew today who would eschew the barbeque in favor of the bugs.

Not eating other humans is simply the food taboo that is most fundamental and universal. Most food taboos are more provincial: some peoples eat pig meat, others don't; some peoples eat dog meat, others don't; some peoples eat insects or poisonous puffer fish or Twinkies or whatever weird things happen to be in their environment and might be nutritious, tasty, or fun to eat. This is not a biological universe, contrasting things that are healthy and filling and digestible to things that aren't; but a symbolic universe, contrasting things that are considered proper and acceptable to be eaten to things that aren't.

Symbolic boundaries are fundamental to human thought, but of course they are imaginary. Those boundaries are crucial to group identity, and they may be cast in terms of what is considered appropriate self-adornment, or how to communicate properly—that is to say, the "boundary work" of culture. In this case, however, the symbolic boundary lies not between those who wear saris and those who wear blue jeans, or between those who distinguish between the "s" sound and the "sh" sound and those who don't—but between those who count as human and those who don't. The widespread rule is this: Animals eat people; people don't.

One of the most striking expressions of this distinction can be found in the process of giving birth, which differs in some key ways between apes and humans. Usually a pregnant ape squats, and since her infant's head is smaller than a human infant's head, she discharges the child quietly and alone. Then she proceeds to eat the placenta and umbilicus. Human mothers do not; in fact the only culture anthropologists know of in which human mothers sometimes do consume the placenta is that of modern urban Californians (and their acolytes). Actress January Jones made gossip headlines when she revealed to *People* magazine that after giving birth in 2011, she had the placenta dried and made into capsules, which she regularly consumed afterward.[9]

It's cool. It's hip. It's natural. For monkeys, that is. Humans generally have someone ritually dispose of the placenta (because there is someone else there, because for humans giving birth is so much harder than it is for other primate species). Like eating a cat, there is no biological reason why you can't do it; you simply consider it disgusting and eat normal food instead. The reason that humans all over the world don't eat their placentas is symbolic: the act is cannibalistic. And the reason that the placenta is disposed of carefully and governed by ritual and taboo is that it is more like a human corpse than like a porterhouse steak.

Human corpses are, of course, universally treated ritually. There are rare cases in which part of the ritual involves eating a bit of the deceased, but that simply goes to show how symbolically charged life and death are.[10] According to the ancient Greeks, the Titan Kronos ate his children (who eventually became the gods), and of course they were not human. But when it comes to human heroes, like Achilles, there are certainly plenty of threats—Achilles stands over mortally wounded Hector and tells him that in his rage he could butcher and eat him on the spot[11]—but of course he won't. That has been the norm in human war since then too: you may inflict horrible indignities upon your enemies, but you refrain from eating them, because that says something beyond horrible about you. Of course, if you want to convince others that you aren't human, that's also a pretty effective way to get their attention.

A dead human body is a symbolically powerfully charged object. Most cultures have taboos about even touching it, much less eating it. But of course, humans don't leave their corpses out, but dispose of them, as they do the placenta. The disposal may involve defleshing, burying, burning, preserving, praying, feasting, or other kinds of practices, and may vary with the status of the deceased—but the dead body is treated ritualistically, not naturalistically. There is plenty of protein to be had in both the new life and the new death, but humans don't avail themselves of it. Where people normatively eat human flesh, it is generally in medicinal or ritual doses, not as a source of nutrition.

That would be yucky, and it just ain't proper. This is the symbolic life of human beings.[12]

INCEST AND THE ORIGIN OF THE FAMILY

Not only are there certain foods that you cannot eat, even though they are edible, but there are also certain people that you cannot marry or have sex with, even though they may be really hot and may love you. Let's start with your mother. Once again, the New Yorker who enjoins you to "eat me, motherfucker!" is not intending to pay you a compliment. Invoking the incest taboo is a powerful insult pretty much everywhere.

The people who are covered by the taboo may vary somewhat from place to place. As noted above, your first cousin may be either a preferred partner or a taboo partner. Your first cousin may even be both—your mother's brother's offspring and your mother's sister's offspring may be considered to be different relations, one a fine mate and the other incestuous. Non-blood relations such as your in-laws may be covered by the same taboos as blood relations. The Bible's incest prohibitions specifically cover a man's stepmother, aunt (i.e., uncle's wife), and daughter-in-law, even though they aren't blood relations.[13]

The origin of these taboos is lost in the dim past. One popular theory has it that the incest taboo is the result of an instinctual program to have a "yecch" reaction to the prospect of intercourse with someone you grew up with.[14] The data invoked here are the low libidos of "child marriages" in China, and the reluctance of Israelis who grow up together on a kibbutz to marry one another.[15] On the other hand, if we are naturally disinclined to mate with those we grow up with, why do we need a cultural taboo to reinforce it? We need cultural rules to stop us from doing things we want to do, not to stop us from doing things we already don't want to do.[16] Further, if the innate disposition is not really strong enough to prevent it from happening—since (1) incest does happen, even normatively;[17] and (2) we apparently need the cultural proscriptions—then what does such an imagined predisposition really explain?

Since the incest taboo is a set of rules (or many sets of rules, with some significant overlaps), we need to account for it principally as such. Where might these rules come from? Sigmund Freud famously focused on the relationship between mother and son as the centerpiece of his explanation: the son desires his mother sexually—the "Oedipus complex"—and so he must be prohibited from consummating that desire. The evidence for that is psychoanalytic, not empirical, however, so it finds few adherents these days.

Primatology, on the other hand, suggests that we look at a different dyad: the relationship between brother and sister. To see why, we need to begin to examine how a human life is different from an ape life. There are two relevant variables to consider: first, the transfer of sexually mature primates out of their natal group; and second, the delayed maturation, especially social maturation, of human beings.

Non-human primates employ a variety of behavioral strategies to minimize inbreeding. By the time a boy baboon is big enough to be socially threatening to the members of his troop, he is booted out, and has to make his way into another troop, where he will live out his adult life. Girl baboons get to stay. It's the opposite for chimpanzees, where females transfer, and males are philopatric; that is, males get to stay with the other chimps they grew up with. Some primates follow the chimp way, others follow the baboon way, and still others combine them. What primates generally don't do is go through puberty with opposite-sex siblings around.[18]

Humans are characterized by slow growth, since so much of our survival depends on learning and socialization. It takes us a couple of years before we can begin to move around properly, and even longer before we can communicate properly; we have far longer periods of immaturity, front-loading the investment in each child against the expectation that it will survive and breed successfully. Thus, where a chimpanzee gets its first adult teeth around age three, a human's first adult tooth does not erupt until around age five. And where a chimp gets its wisdom teeth around age eleven, a human may have to wait twice as long. Indeed in studying human growth, the periods that we divide ape lives into—infants, juveniles, and adults—are simply inadequate to describe the breadth of human development. Human lives need extra divisions to accommodate their longevity and complexity, so we introduce "childhood" between infants and juveniles, and "adolescence" between juveniles and adults.[19]

This slow growth places demands on a human mother that a chimpanzee mother is spared. Let us imagine, for the sake of heuristics, that a chimpanzee mother and a human mother of, say, 100,000 years ago have offspring at approximately equal intervals—say, four years apart. Of course, the human mother has a more difficult time giving birth, and is substantially incapacitated for some time around parturition. Both newborns have four-year-old siblings, for whom mother has to care, although the ape four-year-old is considerably more precocious than the human. Both also have eight-year-old siblings, but here the difference manifests itself more prominently. The eight-year-old chimp is sexually mature and all but independent of its mother, and is being encouraged to leave mother and become socialized into another group (if it is a female). The eight-year-old human is starting fourth grade, still desperately needing mommy. And the twelve-year-old chimp has its wisdom teeth, and is a full-fledged adult; while its human counterpart hasn't even started high school yet.

This all adds up to chimp mommy having a much easier go of it than human mommy. The act of giving birth is easier for the chimpanzee, and she generally only has to worry about caring for two offspring at any given time. Human mommy needs help, and lots of it—and as we will see shortly, it comes from new social relationships. For the time being, however, we have mom taking care of herself, a newborn, a four-year-old, an eight-year-old, and a twelve-year-old. There might even be a sixteen-year-old still hanging around. Obviously she's not doing it alone, and the older kids are helping out with the younger kids, like good humans.

Unlike the chimps, however, who separate at puberty, the human group has teenagers living and associating together as siblings, or at least half sibs. *And if you have opposite-sex teenagers living together, you had better regulate their sexual conduct.*

And that is arguably the basis of the incest taboo: regulating the sexual behavior of opposite-sex siblings in the same family group, a situation that would come to exist far more commonly in humans than in chimpanzees.

And why is that important? Two reasons: First, it represents the origin of morality, of the most basic of human social thought process; there are things you can do and things you can't do, and this is something you can't do. And second, this is also the beginning of the bio-cultural processes of human evolution, the invisible aspects of human evolution, which are lost when we reduce human evolution to simply its biological processes.

THE INVISIBLE ASPECTS OF HUMAN EVOLUTION

By 100,000 years ago, human beings are physically indistinguishable from their modern descendants. With foreheads and chins, their heads are our heads; their bodies and brains are our bodies and brains. They are slightly, but noticeably, different from those of their European contemporaries, the Neanderthals—who lacked foreheads and chins, but otherwise looked very much like ourselves, if we imagine our head without a forehead or chin, and imagine our body as that of a middle linebacker.

Archaeologists can study the material technologies of humans and Neanderthals 100,000 years ago, and find similarities and differences that can speculatively be related to differences in their cognitive function, inferred on account of the elongated heads and brains they had. Of greater interest, however, is the relationship between the humans of then and the humans of now, because the humans of then were cranially the same as us, but behaviorally very different. All their worked, preserved tools were still made of stone—no bone or antler, much less metal. Even something as fundamentally human as drawing—carving and painting—lies tens of thousands of years in the future.

So these were humans who were physically, cranially, cerebrally like us, yet behaviorally very different. Some scholars posit an invisible mutation, a genetic difference that we can't detect, but whose imagined effects render us behaviorally "modern" and distinct from these earlier humans.[20] But that would fly in the face of what we know of modern human behavior—that all people are capable of pretty much of the full range of human activities and mentalities, and their only major differences are due to cultural history, not biology. More consistent with that knowledge is the interpretation that the humans of 100,000 years ago had not yet discovered art, sculpture, and technological diversity—just as they had not yet discovered corn, metals, vacuum cleaners, and cable television. There is consequently nothing anomalous or mysterious about it; they were just on the low end of the great learning curve of human behavior.[21]

These humans of 100,000 years ago were behaviorally far more similar to Neanderthals than to us. Prior to this time, our ancestors were becoming increasingly reliant upon transforming raw materials into tools for their survival, but their stone tools tell us precious little about them. These early people mark the transition between the biological evolution that principally characterized hominid evolution for the previous few million years, and the cultural evolution that principally characterizes it now. This was the age of bio-cultural evolution, when changes in human social behavior entered a complex feedback loop with the natural variables in human life. Those natural variables are the life history traits—rooted in the biological slowdown of development in the human—that coevolved with the cultural and social life of the species.

Unfortunately, however, those aspects of the social and cultural life of early humans are far more difficult to access in the fossil record, and therefore to discuss scientifically, than the features of the body, which form the bedrock of our scientific narratives of human evolution. Consequently, we have a strong tendency to ignore the bio-cultural evolution of humans, and reduce it to merely biological evolution.

Consider, as a case in point, the incest taboo, which provoked this discussion. Most contemporary scientific treatments of the phenomenon treat it as a form of inbreeding avoidance, rather than as a form of morality. Why? Because inbreeding is something that can be measured and compared to other species, while morality is not. And yet, that treatment fails to explain why a first cousin is so often globally a preferred marriage partner. As the French anthropologist Claude Lévi-Strauss once put it, this is precisely where "the transition from nature to culture is accomplished."[22] Similarly, we discuss the evolution of pair bonding, rather than of marriage; although pair bonding does not yield the set of reciprocal obligations and relationships among families that marriage does.

This is what I mean by saying that human evolution is increasingly bio-cultural evolution. It is not to deny that a taboo against mating with close relatives has a salutary effect upon the coefficient of inbreeding that geneticists can measure, nor to deny that humans are pair bonded to a much greater extent than chimpanzees are. But to fail to address the cultural elements and consequences is to miss what is particularly human about human evolution.[23] The efficiency that technology provides had to coevolve with the codes for its appropriate and inappropriate use, for the development of new and efficient ways for our distant ancestors to kill things necessitated the development of rules governing and regulating the practice of killing.[24] And of course, we still see that today, as modern ethical codes strive to keep up with technological innovations.

THE BIO-CULTURAL EVOLUTION OF HUMAN SOCIAL RELATIONS

Taboos are the most basic elements of the moral life, and morality is the most basic element of human social life. Imposing imaginary divisions upon the chaos of the universe is one of the things that the human mind is very good at. So far we have called attention to the well-known separations between the edible things that you can and can't eat, and the sexy people you can and can't have sex with. Normal people respect those boundaries, which identifies them as at least minimally acceptable community members. To fail to respect those boundaries is to identify yourself as someone who would do pretty much anything, that is to say, as being morally dubious, an unpredictable and undesirable kinsman, neighbor, or citizen.

Here, however, we reach an impasse in the study of human evolution. We have entered the realm of collective thought, of relationships among humans, rather than of the properties of humans. These will be crucial to the evolutionary emergence of the human condition, but they will not be physically evident. And since they are not physically evident, they are not part of the database on human evolution.

We have already noted the emergence of the bond between opposite-sex siblings, which is special to humans, for it creates a new kind of social relationship: a lifelong intimate interaction between opposite-sex individuals that is not sexual. This will be symbolically extendable in three ways: first, to other family members, and banning sexual relations with them, once there is a concept of the family; second, to other opposite-sex community or clan members, accompanying a broader conception of kinship than just the family, and forming the basis of exogamous marriage rules;[25] and third, to other generations, where the offspring of those same taboo opposite-sex siblings will be cross-cousins, and may be symbolically special, but in the directly opposite way, as normative spouses. We can take these up in turn.

The family constitutes an invention as significant as cooking and art in human evolution, and is generally underrepresented in our scientific narratives, because it is composed of relationships, rather than of organic properties that leave a material record. To see where it came from, we have to return to the life history of early humans, and the difficult childbirth, and all of those immature offspring. Human motherhood is both continuous with, and discontinuous from, primate motherhood generally. Not only is giving birth necessarily social in humans, because it generally can't be done alone, but that very social aspect means that a human mother is obliged to be more tolerant of others being around her newborn than an ape mother is. Whether it is the newborn's aunts, older siblings, father, or grandparents, or non-relatives, like an obstetrician, midwife, doula, wet nurse, or babysitter, there are far more people in contact with a young human than an ape mother would ever tolerate around her child. Anthropologist Sarah Hrdy has argued that this tolerance of "others" by early human mothers translated outward to the general prosociality (i.e., niceness) of humans, compared to apes.[26]

Two "others" are particularly significant in human evolution, not just for their impact on the material well-being of mother and offspring, but for their social and symbolic aspects as well. The first is the husband (of a woman) or father (of a child)—two relationships, neither of which exists in the apes, embodied in a single person. An ape female might have a pair-bonded male, but a husband is the product of the cultural act of marriage; and an ape child certainly has a genitor, and might even have an adult male around who will tolerate it, but a father is the result of culturally recognized obligations.[27]

Husband/father is thus a bio-cultural status, which can be reduced neither to the biological resident or pair-bonded male nor to the biological sperm donor or caregiver. At issue is the origin of marriage, which is a set of reciprocal obligations between two families. Unlike pair bonding, marriage hardly ever involves just two people, and creates the new social relationships of in-laws, which don't exist among the apes. Marriage is the basis of kinship; it legitimizes sexual relations and gives a child a place in the social order.[28] In addition to the insults evoked by cannibalism and incest, calling someone a bastard is also widely effective cross-culturally, for it suggests that they have no real place in kin-based society. Marriage serves other functions as well—it may establish a new residential unit, economic unit, and political unit, and formalize emotional ties, as well as legalizing reproduction. With so many functions, no wonder it takes so many diverse forms across human cultures.[29] This also makes it very difficult to know just what its original function was. The other "other" is his mother-in-law, of whom more later.

HUMAN EVOLUTION AND MATE CHOICE

A second feature of human society is exogamy, the prescriptive rule to marry someone unrelated to you. This is different from the incest taboo, which is the proscriptive rule against sex with a family member. Exogamy involves recognizing kinship beyond the family, and classifying people as eligible marriage partners or not, largely independently of any meaningful genetic relationships. A seventh cousin once removed on your mother's side might be an eligible spouse, while the equivalent relative on your father's side might not be. This is obviously very highly cultural, for it involves marriage, and the imposition of biologically irrelevant distinctions upon groups of people.

In the urban, modern world, the cultural marriage patterns tend in the opposite direction. We tend to marry people whom we perceive to be compatible, which often means people whom we find to be similar to us in culturally defined ways: similar social class, similar political views, similar religious views, similar educational status, common ethnic background. Why do people do this? Two main reasons: the pragmatic desire for a tranquil domestic life, and parental approval.

This, it may be noted, has very little to do with what some Darwin-intoxicated psychologists model as the evolution of "mate choice"—which assumes that potential spouses are independent autonomous actors, and that their only criteria in a partner are aspects of physical beauty. Thus, based on questionnaire data, men have "evolved" to be attracted to women with a waist-to-hip ratio of .67 (that is, the latter two measurements of 36–24–36), and to women with symmetrical, but average, faces. Other studies purport to show that women "evolved" to be attracted to sugar daddies. This effect is strongly correlated with gender inequality, however; and is most readily visible in cultures where women are systematically denied access to resources, and consequently are obliged to marry them.[30] Other claims include the choice of mates on the basis of detecting who might be a good parent to future offspring, a sensitive sexual partner, or a good kisser.[31] Our ancestors were apparently pulled in many different directions.

Actually, however, evolution probably has rather little to do with it. The argument implicating evolution involves the assumption that we compete for mates, usually males for females. Such competition is often expressed in patterns of sexual dimorphism among primates. Baboons, for example, are highly competitive for mates, and the males are considerably larger than the females, because of what Darwin called sexual selection. On this basis, some biologists have argued that we are naturally somewhat polygynous, like those baboons. On the other hand, baboons also have highly dimorphic canine teeth, while the monogamous gibbons do not. On that basis, some biologists have argued that we are naturally somewhat monogamous. Not only that, but humans are sexually dimorphic in ways that have no homologue in our close relatives, most notably, body composition and facial and body hair. This in turn suggests evolutionary processes at work that we cannot use the primates to model, for the patterns are unique to our own lineage.[32]

Those unique evolutionary processes are of course the bio-cultural evolutionary processes by which we became human. Clearly, when the data are taken in full they present a highly ambiguous case for extracting any natural human socio-sexual system by comparison to other species of primates. For a species in which marriage is the norm and families are involved in choosing mates, the traditional modes of competition that we see in primates will be strongly mitigated. One significant and obvious effect of marriage is that it tends to equilibrate the reproductive output of men relative to women, and of men relative to one another. Sure, there is the occasional sultan with 600 children, but the conditions of extreme power and wealth inequalities that make such a situation possible are very rare and ephemeral in human history. The various social rules about who is excluded and included as an appropriate mate have always made it far narrower than a free market; and a good mate is not only fair of face and form, but also from a good family. But what are the criteria of a good family? They are invariably cultural: perhaps wealthy, perhaps honorable, perhaps familiar, or well connected or wise or skilled. With such diverse non-biological criteria, it seems very unlikely that biological evolution has been busily at work in shaping human mate choice.

Consequently, even evolutionary psychologists have belatedly come around to the recognition that that their conclusions are based on a ridiculously narrow sample of the human species, predominantly white, educated, industrialized, rich, and democratic, or WEIRD—and the relationship of this body of research to human evolution is highly dubious.[33]

And yet, once you have prohibited sexual relations with certain members of the opposite sex on the basis of familial relationship or a more obscure cultural rule, you have created a highly non-primate-like world of male-female social relations. Human sexual acts are more tactile, more intimate, erotic, and simply go on longer than their ape homologues.[34] But we have also reciprocally created a social universe in which men and women can associate with one another for reasons other than mating. College students sometimes call this "platonic friendship," but of course it is far broader than that, and gets to the eventual possibility of having an opposite-sex doctor or minister or mentor or confidant or boss. Thus, relationships between men and women are divergent from relationships between male and female apes both sexually and non-sexually; but the very emergence of a concept of non-sexual relationships between opposite-sex adults is peculiarly human.

MULTIGENERATIONALISM

The third feature of human society that emerges from the invention of the family is the recognition of multigenerationalism, and its attendant implications. Where opposite-sex siblings are taboo sexual or marriage partners, they nevertheless often remain in intimate contact for life. Their immediate descendants, first cousins, will come to lie right on the symbolic boundary of the family, sometimes being taboo partners, and sometimes being preferred partners. This is irrespective of their biological relationship, that is, with a 12.5 percent chance of having inherited the identical allele from their common grandparent. When Charles Darwin married Emma Wedgwood, his mother, Susannah, and Emma's father, Josiah, were siblings—and although that kind of genetic calculation had not yet been invented, Darwin knew that his family was inbred, and was very bothered by that fact. He even speculated that inbreeding, whose effects in other species he wrote about, might be the cause of the susceptibility to disease that seemed to haunt his family.[35]

Generational relationships in the opposite direction are rather more interesting, though. Hominid mother needs help. Her children are hard to bear, very immature, and having a special man around is certainly a good way of solving the problems raised by the emergent aspects of human life history. But a few tens of thousands of years ago, something else happens to the human life history, quite possibly a consequence of the success that these forehead-and-chin people came to enjoy as they spoke, organized themselves, and made things.

They began to get old.[36] And unlike female chimpanzees, who essentially breed until they die, female humans reached an age where they stopped breeding, yet continued to live. The evolution of menopause, so to speak, would provide human mothers with an additional, or alternative, source of material assistance. Thus, grandmotherhood would be a new social relationship, in which a postreproductive female could invest in the propagation of her genes in her grandchild, one generation removed from where chimpanzee females place all of their investment.[37]

This, however, sets up a new and powerful conflicting relationship, between husband and mother-in-law. The husband is simply another role for the father, and the mother-in-law is simply another role for the grandmother. With wife-daughter bound both to her mother (from her old family) and to her husband (from her new family), an obvious tension is established in their relationships to the same person. The consequent relationship between husband and mother-in-law is one of the most famously taboo social interactions across the globe, as much the stuff of vaudeville routines and situation comedies as it is a part of traditional native African, Australian, and American social life. Over a century ago, the early anthropologist James Frazer observed that "the awe and dread with which the untutored savage contemplates his mother-in-law are amongst the most familiar facts of anthropology."[38] The taboo is not one of sexuality, but of simple face-to-face interaction, born of competing for the same person's affections. Even the face-to-face interactions are uniquely human, as our prominent eye whites betray our gaze and focus, making human face-to-face interactions just that much more intimate than ape face-to-face interactions.

Mother-in-law also has another crucial social relationship in her other role as grandmother, beyond the simple provisioning and other material assistance to her daughter and to her daughter's children. Chimpanzees and other primates, after all, have grandmothers—but there is nothing discernibly special about that relationship. For humans, though, grandmother-grandchild is a special relationship, often a contrast to the relationship between parent and child. The specialness of that grandparental relationship, and its contrast to the parental relationship, also highlight an important cognitive element in the evolution of kinship bonds.

If we take the characters of the television show *The Simpsons* as our examples, we have three relationships: Lisa to her mother, Marge; Marge to her mother, Jacqueline; and Lisa to her grandmother Jacqueline. Lisa must learn that her relationship to

Marge is equivalent to Marge's relationship to Jacqueline, but different from Lisa's relationship to Jacqueline. That is actually some pretty fancy brainwork. Indeed, it is essentially the gold standard of human cognition—a theory of mind, or the ability to put yourself in someone else's place. Lisa must be able to put herself in Marge's place in order to understand how her mother's relationship to her grandmother differs from her own relationship to her grandmother. That is to say, she has to learn that "my mother is someone else's daughter."

In addition to the nascent "theory of mind" implied by the recognition of the grandparental generation, there are other important implications as well. After all, if mom is someone's daughter, then grandma must be someone's daughter too. Ancestry itself thus emerges from grandmotherhood.

But why stop at great-grandma? After all, she had a mother, who had a mother, who had a mother . . . back into the dim past— we can now have mythic ancestors, which chimpanzees don't have. We can be descended from the eagle or bear, or from the gods and heroes. Moreover, great-grandma is sadly no longer with us, which in turn raises another question that chimpanzees don't grapple with—namely, Where is she? That, in turn, raises the question of death. Chimpanzees appreciate that another chimpanzee's long-term lack of responsiveness is irreversible; once Boo-Boo has ceased to move, he is not going to start moving again. They certainly understand "here" and "not-here," and they understand "beaten into a limp, bloody, motionless pulp," because they do that occasionally. Sometimes, however, they don't even get that message too quickly, and will carry around a dead youngster until its corpse begins to rot.[39]

Humans, on the other hand, have a thing about death—a cultural thing. It sometimes involves a desire never to die or visitations and communications from those who have died or the special qualities of people who have died or how to interact with their remains now that they are dead. Our ancestors were burying their dead by perhaps 100,000 years ago, and some tens of thousands of years later, were beginning to bury them with material objects—things they liked, things they ought to have with them, things that are just pretty.

The multifaceted system that we call religion—incorporating cognitive elements (answering questions about death, for example), social elements (enacted rituals and shared symbolic meanings), affective elements (awe and transcendence), and normative elements (moral codes)—probably coevolved with, and coalesced around, the origin of human society.[40] And since religion tends to be integrated into human life systemically,[41] there seems little need to reduce it to its moral or psychological aspects in order to understand where it came from.[42] The point is that these are all issues that probably eventually emerged more or less automatically in the minds of cogitating primates engaging with grandmothers, fathers, and siblings.

CHAPTER SEVEN

Human Nature/Culture

As new forms of sociality become increasingly important in the survival and proliferation of humans, brain size becomes proportionally less important. Brain size had been increasing for 2 million years or so, as bipedal primates with chimp-sized brains and cruddy tools came to have remote descendants with brains three times as large and very fine tools. But by perhaps 20,000 years ago something different is going on: the evolution of culture has assumed a trajectory largely independent of the bodies producing it. As the Acheulean tools of 500,000 years ago evolved into the Mousterian tools of 100,000 years ago, the heads and brains of the people using them also evolved. Yet as the biplanes of a century ago evolved into the jetliners of today, they did so without any concomitant change in the brains or heads of the people making or using them. Brain size simply stops being meaningful for human existence, because our survival increasingly becomes predicated on what is between those brains, rather than what is within them—the social aspects of human existence that are invisible paleontologically.[1] These incorporate new un-ape-like ways of perceiving and interacting with relatives and non-relatives, and make the case for human evolution being largely inaccessible to the biologist or primatologist without acknowledging the exceptional elements of our social and cultural history.[2]

As the cultural aspects of our existence increasingly determine the content of our lives—from the languages we speak to our diets, our personal appearance, our thought processes, and most fundamentally, our ability to thrive and breed—it becomes increasingly difficult to separate the natural from the cultural. Indeed, perhaps the most frustrating assertion in the study of human evolution (aside from the claim that it didn't happen) is the claim that there is a "human nature" that is separable from human culture, and discernible on its own—as if culture were like the icing on a cake, simply needing to be scraped off, in order to observe our purely biological selves. But this is wrong for three reasons.

First, we see the human species culturally. Science is a process of understanding, and we understand things culturally. We hope that we can observe and transcend the cultural biases of our predecessors, but there is no non-cultural knowledge. As a graphic example, consider the plaque that was attached to *Pioneer 10*, launched in 1972, and is now outside of our solar system (fig. 2).

Why was NASA sending pornography into outer space? Because they wanted to show the aliens just who it was that had sent the space probe out. But of course the handsome, fit man and woman depicted didn't send the probe out; that was a bunch of male nerds. So the illustration is a symbolic representation of the group that sent the probe out. But which group? Americans? Aerospace engineers? Primates? No, the group NASA wanted to represent was the species *Homo sapiens*. Not children, not seniors, just handsome adults. And why send them naked? After all, that's not

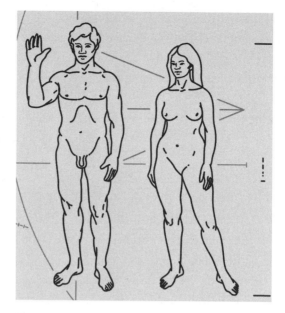

Figure 2. Image from NASA's Pioneer plaque
(Wikimedia Commons).

what the aliens will see when they track the probe back to earth (a
map was also conveniently provided). Answer: Because they
wanted to depict the man and woman in a cultureless, natural
state. But surely the shaves, haircuts, and bikini waxes are cultural! As are the gendered postures, with only the man looking
you straight in the eye. In a baboon, that would be a threat display;
let's hope the aliens who intercept the space probes aren't like
baboons. And finally, what's the caption for the image of the man
with his hand up? "Howdy!—And welcome to our solar system!"
Or "Halt!—This is a private nudist sector of the galaxy!" Or perhaps even, "Excuse me, but is there a bathroom in this quadrant?"

Thus, in believing itself to be freeing the image of culture,
NASA was really filling it with cultural information, but simply

failing to recognize it. Culture is always there, in human thought and act, and it is very easy to mistake for nature.

Second, we have been coevolving with culture for a very long time, several millions of years. There seems little doubt that dexterity and intelligence and technology all coevolved. Culture is thus, in a very fundamental sense, an ultimate cause of the human condition: we have evolved to be adapted to it.

And third, the environment in which we grow and develop is fundamentally a cultural one, filled with social relationships, linguistic meanings, manual labor, prep school, fatty beef and high fructose corn syrup, beer, smog, and cigarettes. Culture is thus also a proximate cause of the human condition. To talk of human nature abstracted from culture is pre-Darwinian nonsense. From the standpoint of human evolution, then, the quest to discover a human nature independent of human culture is a fool's errand; human facts are invariably natural/cultural facts.

OUR SPECIES, OURSELVES

The fallacy of reducing natural/cultural facts to natural facts lies behind the long-standing fallacy of race—the idea that the human species can be naturally partitioned into a fairly small number of fairly discrete kinds of people. Race was the first question that guided anthropology in the eighteenth century: given that there were all these natural kinds of animals, vegetables, and minerals out there, what natural kinds of people were there?

At the conjunction of the age of exploration, the age of colonialism, and the age of science, the Swedish biologist Carl Linnaeus gave a definitive scientific answer: there are four kinds of people, living on different continents, and color coded for your convenience—white Europeans, yellow Asians, red Americans, and black Africans. And they could be naturally separated not simply on the basis of their continents and colors, but also on the basis of how they dressed (tight-fitting clothes, loose-fitting clothes, painting themselves with fine red lines, and anointing themselves with grease, respectively) and their legal system (law, opinion, custom, and whim, respectively).[3]

The next generation of scholars tried to rely more on simply physical attributes, and also synonymized Linnaeus's taxonomic category of "subspecies" with a more colloquial term referring to a strain or lineage of living things—race. In practice that meant that two usages of the term were concurrent—in reference to (1) a formal taxonomic subspecies, and (2) an informal group of people sharing a common identity and narrative of descent. The first would remain, with minor modifications, the classification of Linnaeus; the second, however, would allow you to racialize groups like the Gypsies, Lapps, Eskimos, and Jews (now known as the Roma, Sami, Inuit, and Jews). By the 1920s, anthropologists were arguing that the latter kind of race was largely illusory, for those groups were not "natural" units; and by the 1960s, anthropologists were coming around to the realization that the first kind of race was illusory as well. Early fieldwork showed, for example, that continental groups were far from homogeneous. Thus, works like *The Races of Africa* and *The Races of Europe* showed that however earnestly the investigators believed themselves to be looking at large natural subdivisions of the human species, those subdivisions could themselves be readily subsubdivided.[4]

As early as 1931, the biologist Julian Huxley would observe, "It is a commonplace of anthropology that many single territories of tropical Africa, such as Nigeria or Kenya, contain a much greater diversity of racial type than all Europe."[5] Nearly twenty years later, when Huxley was president of UNESCO, he commissioned a Statement on Race to formalize and disseminate the post–World War II consensus. Change did not come so easily, however, and scholars of the earlier generation, including some former Nazi anthropologists, objected strongly to the newer consensus.[6] Nevertheless, as we noted in chapter 1, by 1957 we now understood the human species "as constituting a widespread network of more-or-less interrelated, ecologically adapted and functional entities."[7]

The modern understanding of human variation that emerged in the later part of the twentieth century involved a new empirical understanding of human variation, implying that race, like the geocentric solar system, was effectively an optical illusion. You could see human races much as you could see the sun rise, cross the sky, and set over the opposite horizon; but your mind was simply playing tricks on you. In one case, the earth's rotation leads you to embrace the geocentric illusion; in the other case, centuries of political intellectual history lead you to embrace the racial illusion.

The major features of human diversity are patterned quite differently than Linnaeus and two subsequent centuries of premodern human science thought. The primary ways that human groups are similar or different from one another is cultural, although that concept only began to be formalized in the 1870s. If we (perversely) choose to ignore the primary patterns of human diversity, and try to focus instead only on the biological differences, we find that the major pattern of human biological diversity is polymorphism; that is to say, most alleles in the human gene pool are cosmopolitan, and found in most places, although in varying proportions. The second UNESCO statement on race, released in 1951, explained that for observable features, "the differences among individuals belonging to the same race are greater than the differences that occur between the observed averages for two or more races," but it was not until 1972 that the geneticist Richard Lewontin was able to quantify that statement by studying genetic data. He was able to show that upward of 80 percent of the detectable genetic data in the human species was to be found within any individual population—a finding that has proven to be robust to all kinds of genetic data.[8] If you choose to ignore the cultural and the polymorphic variation, the major feature that remains is clinal, that is to say, varying gradually over geography. And if you choose to ignore the cultural, the polymorphic, and the clinal, what's left is local variation. Race is simply a biological illusion.[9]

But knowing what race is not doesn't tell us what race is. Race is a process of aggregating and classifying people, creating bounded categories of difference where none exist "out there." It is thus a conjunction of difference and meaning. That is to say, you can measure how different people are, or populations are, but that does not tell you whether they constitute two variations on the same theme, as it were, or two different themes. Those decisions involve the construction and imposition of meaning upon the patterns of human diversity you observe, the attribution of different properties to people on either side of the boundaries, as well as the patrolling of those boundaries (in the form of miscegenation laws).

The recognition that race is a fact of nature/culture, rather than a fact of nature, is sometimes misunderstood. In a reductive mind-set that sees biological, or even genetic, facts as real, and cultural facts as less real, we sometimes hear that we now know that race "is not real." But natural facts are often less real than cultural facts—like money or education. Facts of nature are usually not very important to human existence any more: that has been the trajectory of human evolution for the last few million years—to create our environments and realities. Indeed, as a unit of nature/culture, race can be a crucial determinant of the attributes of one's life. Race can be inscribed upon the body in remarkably subtle ways, for example, where apparently consistent racial differences in biomedical risk factors often turn out to be a result of the conditions of life.[10] As it has been epigrammatically noted, your zip code is a better predictor of your health risks than your DNA code.

THE RELATION BETWEEN HUMAN MICROEVOLUTION AND MACROEVOLUTION

One can, of course, study the differentiation of human populations—how they specialize and survive and adapt to local conditions. They do it culturally, physiologically, and genetically, and usually all at the same time. Geneticists, however, sometimes try to bracket their own data and analyze the genetics separately, often in the naive belief that in so doing, their work is free of the cultural constraints and values entailed in working on people.

That is what the earliest students of the blood groups thought. With the discovery of the ABO system, geneticists in World War I tried to cluster the human species into natural groups and discern the true "races of mankind." They concluded that there were three kinds of people: European, Intermediate, and Asio-African—or essentially "white" and "other."[11] They sampled more populations and analyzed more loci, but kept coming up with racial nonsense. Into the 1960s, in fact, one leading proponent of racial genetics could claim to have identified thirteen human races, including five in Europe and only one in Africa—hardly indicative of anything uncultural. It wasn't until a decade later that the geneticists came to realize that their data don't actually reveal races at all; like the rest of the data on human biological diversity, they universally exposed polymorphic, clinal, and local variation.[12]

There is, of course, geographic differentiation of peoples and their gene pools. There are also discontinuities of greater or lesser extents, caused by features like mountain ranges or language difference; and statistical ways of discerning them. But none of them produce the fairly large and fairly discrete kinds of people that we encode as "races." (One famous study, which was widely misrepresented, divided the human gene pool into between two and seventeen groups, the actual number being input rather than discovered. When it partitioned the human gene pool into five groups it retrieved essentially continental groupings, and into six groups it retrieved the continents and the Kalash people of Pakistan.[13])

The recognition, in the third quarter of the twentieth century, that microevolutionary taxonomy did not describe a significant biological component of the human species, for our species had a very different empirical structure, was paralleled by new insights in macroevolutionary human taxonomy. By the 1970s, paleontology had collapsed many of the old, weird genera (like *Plesianthropus, Pithecanthropus, Telanthropus,* and *Zinjanthropus*) into just two: *Homo* and *Australopithecus.* (*Paranthropus* would later be resurrected for the "robust australopithecines.")

The historian Robert Proctor has observed that the microevolutionary and macroevolutionary taxonomies are intertwined, for the practice "is ultimately a moral choice.... As cultural creatures, we have the capacity to determine whom we will include or exclude as part of us."[14] The proliferation of taxa below and above the species level constructs a narrow channel for entry into "us-ness."

Milford Wolpoff and Rachel Caspari have called attention to the links between the scientific philosophy of essentialism in understanding prehistory and modern human diversity. "Essentialism" is a term that does a lot of work in philosophy of science, and in the present context it means establishing biological groups on the basis of its members possessing one or a few key features. Any specimen or person lacking the crucial feature must therefore be accommodated by establishing a new category. This practice, they argue, promotes the proliferation of pigeonholes, which in turn easily become tree branches, and give the illusion that they can be linked into a phylogenetic history.[15] In short, the process of biological reification above the species level is connected to biological reification below it.

NEANDERTHALS AND THE BOUNDARY OF MICRO- AND MACROEVOLUTION

The Neanderthals hold a special place—biologically and mythologically—in the knowledge of who we are and where we came from.[16] The discovery of Neanderthals in the nineteenth century pointed to a deep history of "otherness" in Europe, of people who might have been victims, variants, or even ancestors of modern-day Europeans.[17] Their differences from us are fairly small. Their brains were the same size as ours, but the heads that contained them were low and long. You can find people today with brow ridges or sloping foreheads or weak chins or long heads or large, narrow faces or projecting midfaces or large jaws with more than enough room for wisdom teeth. But you don't find those features together, or quite so extreme, in anyone living today.

What, then, is our relation to the Neanderthals? Are "they" the odd-looking people whom "we"—that is to say, lanky, round-headed, anatomically modern *Homo sapiens*—dispossessed and exterminated? That was an explanation that made sense to nineteenth-century Europeans, who eagerly imagined their own colonial ambitions and barbaric exterminations stretching back into the dim past.[18] Or did "they" represent humans in a state of pure nature, their lives "solitary, poore, nasty, brutish and short" as Thomas Hobbes and his Enlightenment successors portrayed the forerunners—and shadow—of civil society? Perhaps "they" were neither primordial victims nor primordial forebears, but simply freaks of nature—deformed, maybe by accident of birth or circumstance of life, and interesting because they are weird and pathological.[19]

The truth is likely to be "a little of each," since the alternatives were never mutually exclusive. Their bones show lots of evidence of healed fractures; their teeth are worn as if they were being used as tools; and their muscular development was strikingly asymmetrical. Whatever they did, it was rigorous, it was cultural, and it was humane (at least, they took care of friends with broken arms better than chimpanzees do). They also tended to get a lot more exercise on one side than the other. They were replaced in the fossil record of Europe by less stocky people like you and me, who had chins and foreheads. And yes, they were uncivilized. They sometimes buried their dead, but never sent any grave goods along with the deceased for the journey. They didn't build anything, or at least anything lasting or recognizable. If they decorated themselves, or had any aesthetic sensibility at all, it was rudimentary at best.

The imaginary encounter between a human and a Neanderthal has been the subject of a wide range of literary efforts, from Jack London (*Before Adam*) and William Golding (*The Inheritors*) to the contemporary novelists Jean Auel (*The Clan of the Cave Bear*) and Robert J. Sawyer (*Hominids*). What stimulates the imagination is the encounter with otherness; after all, it was only in 1537, in a papal bull called *Sublimus Dei,* that Pope Paul III officially declared that Native Americans were actually rational beings with souls. So what would it be like to encounter someone who was so different from you that they might possibly be considered not really human?

Of course, we don't know—but we do know that our answers to the seemingly natural question "Human or not?" are strongly conditioned culturally. Where naturalists of the eighteenth century appreciated that the interfertility of living peoples everywhere indicated that we were all one species, slavers of the ninteenth century worked hard to inflict a subhuman condition upon their victims, and then to read that as an indication of their subhuman natures. By the twentieth century, reactionary geneticists tried to show that there might be hidden debilitating effects of interracial matings.[20] As late as the 1950s, a right-wing botanical geneticist named Reginald R. Ruggles Gates would argue that since plants are profligate outside their recognized species boundaries, human interfertility should not be a criterion for placing us all in the same species. And in 1962, a physical anthropologist named Carleton Coon sacrificed his career and reputation on a book purporting to show that whites had become human 200,000 years before blacks had.[21] Of course these reactionary works were all influenced by the politics of the age, which is exactly the point.

The politics are more subtle, but Neanderthals have been shuttled back and forth across the boundary of humanity over the years. They have had gender roles projected upon them, been portrayed as cannibals and as flower children,[22] and even been caught up in bioethics discussions—as a geneticist recently glibly called for a "an extraordinarily adventurous woman" to carry a cloned Neanderthal to term.[23] The Neanderthals are a little bit different physically, and a little bit different technologically, but of course we don't know what they were like mentally or socially, and fossils can't mate. So, do we expand the category "human" to include them (as a subspecies, *Homo sapiens neanderthalensis*—in contrast to our own, *Homo sapiens sapiens*), or do we restrict "human" solely to people in our contemporary, modern frame of reference (and call them *Homo neanderthalensis*)? In the 1980s the genetic data were counted strongly in favor of the latter; today they count strongly in favor of the former.[24] What the genetic data will strongly show thirty years hence is anybody's guess. It does seem as though the final call on that question is underdetermined by the science, genetic or anatomical. That is because the issue, the boundary of our species, the fence around humanity, is constructed from nature/culture.

The greatest falsehood of the imaginary encounter between a human and a Neanderthal is that they would be classifying us the way *we* classify us. As if, after emerging from your time machine in 70,000 B.C. and chancing upon a band of early humans, they would greet you with "Hey, it's another one of us forehead-and-chin guys! Come on and sit a while! You like roast mammoth?"

But you don't hang out with people who have same shaped skull as you. Nobody does. Actually, of course, they would probably evaluate you the way people always have and probably always will—they would look to see whether you could communicate and behave appropriately, present yourself appropriately and share basic ideas and values with them, by which they could infer that your behavior is more or less predictable. Since you would have no idea how to communicate or behave, you would probably seem pretty weird, if not threatening. The idea that they would evaluate you based on your chin and forehead is an ethnocentric conceit, and to them you would probably be at least as different as a Neanderthal would be. It's hard not to think of early modern humans as a cohesive unit, different from Neanderthals and aware of it, and behaving accordingly. But it is probably a mistake to constrain our understandings of Pleistocene peoples by encoding our own cultural biases into them.

One important cultural bias involves the fallacy of reification. Why assume that the Neanderthals were a single coherent group, simply because their technologies were similar and their bodies were similar? Again, if they were like other cultural groups—like us, that is—then they probably exploited local resources differently across space and time, communicated differently, and acted differently. The idea that they were somehow a single cultural unit, because we identify them as such skeletally, is actually a bit of a stretch. Consider the Aryans: Once upon a time there was a philologist at Oxford named Max Mueller. He mastered Sanskrit and ancient Indian scriptures and wrote popular works about the early Indian nobility called Aryas, and inferred that they were the original speakers of the ancestral Indo-European language, which he called Aryan. And pretty soon his acolytes were not only talking about the Aryan-speakers but about the people doing the speaking—their attributes, both cultural and physical. Toward the end of his life he famously chastised those followers of his who were so aggressively reifying the Aryans.

I have declared again and again that if I say Aryans, I mean neither
blood nor bones nor hair nor skull; I mean simply those who speak
an Aryan language.... I commit myself to no anatomical characteristics.... To me an ethnologist who speaks of Aryan race, Aryan
blood, Aryan eyes and hair, is as great a sinner as a linguist who
speaks of a dolichocephalic dictionary or a brachycephalic gram-
mar. To me it is worse than a Babylonian confusion of tongues—it
is downright theft.[25]

The point is that he appreciated that he was talking about a
deduced language, and although someone had to be speaking it,
and they had to look like something, those deductions were considerably removed from the data, which were simply inferences
about an old language family that he was calling Aryan. And we
all know where that went a couple of generations later. So
anthropologists are wary of reifying peoples.

Yet we impose modern cultural ideas not only upon the life
of Neanderthals, but upon their death, too. The most frequent
question we ask about the Neanderthals is, Why did they
become extinct? Why didn't they make it, as we did?[26] As
framed, the question invites you to identify the flaw in Neanderthals, why they missed out on "The preservation of favoured
races in the struggle for life," as Darwin's subtitle to *The Origin of
Species* had it. What, in short, was wrong with them? We have
quite a list of candidate flaws: too dumb, too uncommunicative,
too carnivorous, too cold adapted, too pacifist, too conservative,
just too damn ugly. And yet we don't ask that question about
other former human groups. What was wrong with the Hittites?
What was wrong with the Sumerians? What was wrong with
the Olmec? If they had empires, their empires rose and fell.
But we see the people themselves as part of the ebb and flow of
human bio-culturally constituted social units—assuming iden-

tities, having identities imposed upon them, leaving their graves and objects behind, and leaving behind relatives with other identities.

Descent and relatedness are bio-cultural, and are aspects of a unifying theory, kinship—which is a universally mythologized biology. The status of skeletal remains from Liang Bua (*"Homo floresiensis"*) are disputed, but why should it be particularly important to the science of human evolution if there was once an island of isolated, late-surviving primitive hominids in Indonesia?[27] What would they actually change our ideas of? The "hobbits" would be interesting as newfound cousins, as a part of our narrative of deep kinship and descent. With the "hobbits" the myth is only slightly different, at best; but the new mythologies of *Homo floresiensis* have far surpassed their scientific value. And thus, even as the Neanderthals are being progressively demythologized in the old ways, new mythologies of human origins are taking form.

MEET THE DENISOVANS

The problem of imposing macroevolutionary taxonomic thought upon human microevolution is seen in modern controversies about the "Denisovans." Who were the Denisovans? A race of mighty Ice Age hunters, who traversed the great frozen steppes with steely resolve, looked the great woolly mammoths straight in the eye, and thrived by their wits and cunning in those dark, primordial, and savage times.

Actually, they were a finger bone and a couple of teeth, dated to about 50,000 years ago, from a single stratigraphic layer in a cave in Siberia. And with the aid of high technology and low theory, we have learned a little about them. Initially, the mitochondrial DNA isolated from the finger bone indicated that the finger bone was genetically distinct from both Neanderthal finger bones and modern human finger bones.[28] Thus, the finger bone quickly became a genome, a body, a gene pool, and a population: the Denisovans. Soon thereafter, the nuclear DNA of said digit was sequenced, and it showed the Denisovans to be a divergent offshoot of the Neanderthals.

So far, so good. There's no reason why a 50,000-year-old-hominid from Siberia should closely match a human or a Neanderthal, while being very generally similar to both. Nor is there a reason why mitochondrial and nuclear DNA results should perfectly coincide, since they are transmitted differently. After all, nuclear DNA is transmitted biparentally via the chromosomes. Mitochondrial DNA (mtDNA) is transmitted only maternally. This means that you are chromosomally equally closely related to your mother and father; but mitochondrially a clone of your mother and unrelated to your father. Moreover, as noted in chapter 1, it means that three generations back, you are a mitochondrial clone of one of your eight great-grandparents, and unrelated to the other seven. Although mtDNA is high tech, it is not tracking ancestry in a commonsensical or normative genetical sense.

But what happens when we compare the DNA of the Denisovans to those of different modern human groups, and use the unique DNA sites to ask our computers to draw trees? Then we discover that although many peoples have a tiny fraction of similarity to Denisova, the people with the greatest similarity are not Asians, but Melanesians, from Papua New Guinea. In fact, geographically, to get from Siberia (where the finger bone is from) to New Guinea (where the greatest genetic similarities to the finger bone are found today), you have to go through a lot of

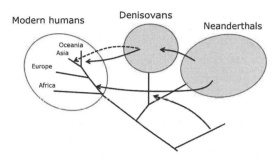

Figure 3. Inferred cladistic relationships and patterns of gene flow among humans, Denisovans, and Neanderthals (after Prüfer et al. 2014).

peoples who have no detectable genetic similarities at all to the Denisovan finger bone.[29]

Then they sequenced a toe bone, from the same stratum but a little bit below the finger bone, and found it to cluster with Neanderthals, not with either the finger bone or modern humans.[30]

And then they sequenced some DNA from a site in Spain, some hundreds of thousands of years earlier than Denisova, and thousands of miles away, and identified some intimate similarities to Denisova.[31] Even more recently, Denisovan DNA has been suggested as the source of genetic adaptations to high altitude in modern Tibetans.[32]

In a cladistic, taxonomic framework, this is very difficult to make sense of (fig. 3).

The diagrams start out with three branches, leading to modern humans, Denisovans, and Neanderthals, respectively. Then the human branch has to start sub-branching, and some of the sub-branches have to connect to the Denisovans. Then things go back and forth to the Neanderthals, and before you know it, you've got not a tree, but a trellis or rhizome, or capillary system. Your mistake was to think that the history you were trying to reconstruct was a tree in the first place.

What is going on over the last few hundred thousand years of human evolution is microevolution, and is thus not dendritic or tree-like. It's a big mystery if you take the trees of similarity to be trees of taxonomic divergence, where groups with names are reified as units of biology. But once we realize that the named human groups are bio-cultural entities, and the Denisovans are reifications, we can reframe the question, and ask why we see this genetic hodgepodge. The answer, of course, is that we are dealing with mobile groups of hunter-gatherers in space and time, demographically complex and genetically connected; and their genetic relationships are not the branches of a tree, but a bowl of ramen noodles.

Some people, and some groups of people, are more genetically similar than others, based on their proximity in space and time. And indeed one can study that, and come up with "genetic distances" and build trees from them. And they can be informative, and can answer intelligent questions put to them. But population geneticists have also been known to draw trees clustering all kinds of human groups. A widely publicized study from 1988 drew a genetic tree that linked together the genomes of national (political) categories (Ethiopian, Iranian, Korean), linguistic categories (Bantu, Uralic, Nilo-Saharan), ethnic categories (Khmer, Eskimo, Ainu), and broad geographic categories (West African, Central Amerindian, European).[33] But these are neither comparable nor natural units. An ambitious population geneticist could cluster Cardinal fans, Blue Jay fans and Tiger fans, and get a tree, and yet would hopefully know that the tree had no biological meaning because the taxa aren't natural units, like cardinals, blue jays, and tigers.

Likewise, the idea that "the Iranians" or "the West Africans" or "the Ainu" constitute some kind of natural, taxonomic unit—much less "the Denisovans"—is a very misleadingly cultural way to think about human microevolution. Biologists generally refer to "reticulate evolution" as a means of describing the striking discordances between macroevolutionary species trees and small bits of genomes that may be distributed strangely, because of crossing between species (especially in plants), or viruses that pick up DNA from one species and put it into another. So in one sense, it's old news.[34] The problem in humans, though, is especially complicated by the pseudo-taxonomic status of human groups. This is not a case of two species that are ordinarily distinct occasionally swapping genetic bits; but rather, two groups of people intimately connected by history and behavior, in spite of having different identities or names. It's the basic confusion of bio-culturally constituted groups being confused with biologically constituted groups.

Good statistics can never correct for bad epistemology.

But there is an interesting mathematical argument to show just how biologically meaningless it is, indeed, to try to link these DNA sequences from tens of thousands of years ago to one another and to particular living people. There are over 7 billion people alive now. They each have two parents. Yet a generation ago, there weren't 14 billion people on earth? Why not? Because most of those parents are common ancestors. Two siblings don't have four parents; they have two parents. Two first cousins don't have eight total grandparents; they have six. And that is why fifty generations ago, say, in the Middle Ages, you had 2^{50} ancestors—or round about a quadrillion, vastly more than the number of people alive back then, or the number of people that have ever lived.

So how do we squeeze the huge number of ancestors that we each have today into the few tens of millions or so people that were alive back then? The answer is that nearly all of them are common ancestors. That is how we are all inbred, and all related to one another—because the vast majority of our ancestors are (1) recurring many times in our own pedigrees; and (2) held in common with everyone else we know.

What we are describing here is called pedigree collapse, by demographers and genealogists.[35] What it means is that, even in fairly recent historic times, nearly everyone is related to (that is, they share common ancestors with) everybody else.[36] And this would only be exacerbated by population crashes due to plagues, as well as the universal human tendency to mate non-randomly with people who match them linguistically and ethnically.

Now the interesting mathematical question: How far back in time would you have to go in order to essentially statistically guarantee that everyone alive today has common ancestors? And the answer: Surprisingly recently, only 5,000 or 10,000 years.[37]

So Og, back in the Upper Pleistocene of 20,000 years ago, is an ancestor either of nobody alive today (his whole family might have been killed in an avalanche, after all) or of everybody alive today. Of course, certain particular ancestors recur more in some people's genealogies than in other people's genealogies. But nobody living 20,000 years ago was the lineal ancestor of only some people alive today.

So where does that leave our friends, the Denisovans from Siberia 50,000 years ago, in connection with living human peoples? Here, the population genetics seems to be at odds with the molecular genetics. We find a few percentage points of similarity when we isolate the unique nucleotides of Denisovan genome and match them up against modern people—and we find them more commonly in Melanesia than in Asia.

The solution to this apparent conundrum is probably that genetic descent is meaningless that far back in time. The connection between people 50,000 years ago and modern peoples is a series of bubbles percolating out of a diverse ancestral brew of human gene pools, all connected to one another in various ways, and to varying extents.[38] If you biologically reify modern human groups, and imagine the ancient groups to be separate taxonomic entities as well, you can get answers. But those answers probably have little or no biological meaning in the context of the descent of modern people from the people of 50,000 years ago.

So what genealogical sense do we make of being told by recreational genetic testing companies that your DNA is, say, 2.4 percent Neanderthal and 3.1 percent Denisovan? Two percent may sound like a little bit, only two in a hundred, but remember that 50,000 years ago you had an astronomically high number of lineal ancestors, who were crammed into bodies of everybody else's physical ancestors. The differences among living peoples in terms of their descent from those people of 50,000 years ago are quantitative, not qualitative. Those differences reside in how many times in each person's pedigree any particular ancient ancestor recurs; we are all descended from the same ancestors, but some more than others. Consequently, we don't need to imagine marauding bands of Ice Age rapists—or even a genetically equivalent, but nicer image—but only a loose network of diverse human gene pools, connected over time and through space, of which we all partake today, if slightly unevenly.

CONCLUSION

There are many ways to think about descent and relatedness, and none of them is objective and uncultural. And although we usually think of the cultural study of kinship as applying to families and clans and totemic ancestors, those generalizations apply as well to *Homo sapiens* and its descent from *Australopithecus afarensis* and its relation to *Pan troglodytes*. Some ways of thinking about it are more or less constrained by the available data: skeletal, archaeological, primatological, ethnographic, historical. The engagement with our ancestors and relatives is necessarily accompanied by a reflexivity that makes this science different from, and often unfamiliar to, scientists trained in other fields.

We often hold out the hope that genomics will answer the important evolutionary questions of the age. But we do that for cultural reasons, the result of decades of propaganda for the Human Genome Project, which even has a name, geno-hype.[39] Genetics is the scientific study of heredity, and needs to be aggressively differentiated from the idea that heredity is the most important factor in one's life, although those two ideas have been widely conflated, often by geneticists themselves, over the course of the twentieth century. Where genetics is problem driven ("How does heredity work?"), genomics is driven often by financial and technological concerns. The Human Genome Project was begun on the promise of curing genetic disease, but its primary advances have been in diagnostics and forensics. In evolutionary anthropology, however, genomics cannot answer the most basic question: Why aren't we apes? Nor will it ever be able to; for the answer to that question lies as much within the social/historical realm as within the genomic/biological realm.

The contested boundary of the human species itself allows us to use it as a basis for understanding the unique contribution of anthropology to the study of the human condition: that human biological facts are never natural facts, but are natural/cultural facts. That is to say, they are not discovered, but are the result of a complex negotiation among what seems to be "out there"; what ideas we bring to the endeavor of describing, understanding, explaining it; and our own perceived rational interests in how to present and utilize it. Misrepresenting facts of human biology as natural facts has historically been the source of ostensibly scientific justifications for conservative political policies.

Consequently, the principal struggle of modern evolutionary theory is to distance itself from odious political views that invoke evolution to claim scientific legitimacy. According to a conservative scholar in 2007, "Conservatives need Charles Darwin.... The intellectual vitality of conservatism in the 21st century will depend on the success of conservatives in appealing to advances in the biology of human nature as confirming conservative thought." Here, "human nature" means little more than imaginary organic limits to social progress.

Those imaginary limits are often more visible to non-scientists. *The Origin of Species,* written in 1859, can still be read without grimacing, specifically because Darwin avoided talking about people in it. And when he finally got around to talking about people, over a decade later, in *The Descent of Man,* we can see now that it is filled with sexist Victorian claptrap. Indeed, somewhat later, in 1922, when politician William Jennings Bryan came out against evolution in an op-ed in the *New York Times,* he specifically highlighted the sexism he identified in Darwin's later work:

> Darwin explains that man's mind became superior to woman's because, among our brute ancestors, the males fought for the females and thus strengthened their minds. If he had lived until now, he would not have felt it necessary to make so ridiculous an explanation, because woman's mind is not now believed to be inferior to man's.[40]

This is particularly ironic in light of the scandal that enveloped Larry Summers, the president of Harvard almost a century later, after addressing the question of why there were so few women on the senior science faculty at institutions like his own. His answer was that perhaps they lacked the intrinsic aptitude at the high end. Maybe it's true; maybe there are occult mental forces found more commonly in men that dispose them toward tenure in science. But how would we know, unless we examine the institutionalized practice of science faculty tenuring at Harvard and elsewhere? Maybe the problem is the pipeline itself, rather than its contents. But by invoking imaginary genetic limitations, Summers was suggesting that the problem was not science's or Harvard's, but women's. So if the phenomenon is simply a part of the biology of *Homo sapiens,* then there is really no problem of social or institutional discrimination worth worrying about or examining—a highly bio-political dissimulation masquerading as a scientific fact of human nature. And it's been wrong every other time it's been invoked, so the chances that it's right this time are probably pretty small.

These days, it is not uncommon to hear evolution invoked in support of a range of bio-political claims, of differing degrees of loathsomeness: that there are no truly selfless acts; that it is natural to hate people different from you; that it is natural for men to dig young babes and women to dig sugar daddies; that rape is not a crime of power using sex as a weapon, but just misguided reproductive effort; and that there are different kinds of people and they have different intellectual properties, just deal with it.[41] If you want to know why there is creationism, it's because this crap passes for evolution. And believe me, I have only scratched the surface.

Certainly the human gene pool is still being tweaked in various ways, but it is always easy to overvalue the tweaking.[42] After all, whatever alleles exist for sharp vision and disease resistance are not nearly as important in the modern world as glasses and antibiotics are. The best examples of recent genetic adaptations are not at all "the spread of a good allele." Sickle-cell anemia is a disease, after all, which changes your red blood cell from the shape of a bialy to that of a croissant. It's "good" (in terms of malaria resistance), but only if you have exactly one copy of it, not zero and not two. But the children of people with one copy of the allele don't necessarily have one copy of the allele themselves: they may have zero or two, with neither genotype being optimal. Consequently it is polymorphic everywhere it is found—there is no population in which everyone has the allele. We don't know nearly as much about lactose tolerance, the allele that allows you to eat quiche without getting explosive diarrhea, but it is also polymorphic everywhere. There are no populations composed of entirely quiche eaters. Indeed, the story we have for the main lactase-persistence allele, spreading from southeast Europe to northwest Europe a few thousand years ago from the benefits of being able to drink milk, has to be an oversimplification, since the most-lactose-tolerant peoples are *not* those who were the *first* dairyers (in southeast Europe), but those who became dairyers *last*, in northwest Europe.[43] And the story of an adaptation in human brain alleles, published in *Science* in 2005, was little more than a racist genomic myth.[44] It's enough to make you wonder what motivates scientists to keep looking so hard for evidence of recent favorable genetic adaptations in human populations; just as scientists of generations past looked so hard for reliable evidence linking brain size to intelligence. If it's there, it can't be really important, because we have been looking really hard for a really long time without finding it.

Actually, the human brain, mind, and gene pool are generally remarkably unadapted and plastic, which makes a good deal of sense, given (1) the reliance on adaptability, rather than adaptation, which is the evolutionary hallmark of our lineage;[45] (2) the scope and complexity of the environments to which early human populations were adapting;[46] and (3) the demographics of early human bands, which would have favored the action of genetic drift,[47] opposing the precision engineering of anything, including the brain.

I have argued here that a comprehension of the science of human origins incorporates multiple elements: first, the data and an understanding of how they are produced; second, the connection between how we understand our ancestry (phylogeny) and how we understand ourselves (diversity); third, an acknowledgment of the cultural aspects of human evolutionary theory, a repudiation of its repressive invocations, and a focus on its progressive implications; and fourth, a reflexive engagement with the political, theological, and moral dimensions of origin narratives generally, and eventually with those of the creationists, whom we hope will come to find evolution less culturally threatening, and thus less rejectable, than they have found it over recent decades.

NOTES

PREFACE

1. Franklin, S. 2013. *Biological Relatives: IVF, Stem Cells, and the Future of Kinship*. Durham, NC: Duke University Press.

2. Gee, H. 2013. *The Accidental Species: Misunderstandings of Human Evolution*. Chicago: University of Chicago Press, p. 13.

3. Snow, C. P. 1959. *The Two Cultures and the Scientific Revolution*. London: Cambridge University Press.

CHAPTER ONE. SCIENCE

1. Simpson, G. G. 1966. "The Biological Nature of Man." *Science* 152:472–78.

2. Schneider, D. M. 1968. *American Kinship: A Cultural Account*. Englewood Cliffs, NJ: Prentice-Hall. Franklin, S., and S. McKinnon, eds. 2001. *Relative Values: Reconfiguring Kinship Studies*. Durham, NC: Duke University Press. Carsten, J. 2004. *After Kinship*. New York: Cambridge University Press. Sahlins, M. 2011. "What Kinship Is, Part One." *Journal of the Royal Anthropological Institute* 17:2–19.

3. Dundes, A. 1998. *The Vampire: A Casebook*. Madison: University of Wisconsin Press.

4. Gobineau, A. 1853. *Essai sur l'inégalité des races humaines.* Vol. 1. Paris: Firmin Didot Fréres. Gobineau, A. 1915. *The Inequality of Human Races.* New York: G.P. Putnam's Sons. Poliakov, L. 1974. *The Aryan Myth.* New York: Basic Books.

5. Kale, S. 2010. "Gobineau, Racism, and Legitimism: A Royalist Heretic in Nineteenth-Century France." *Modern Intellectual History* 7:33–61.

6. Snow, C.P. 1959. *The Two Cultures and the Scientific Revolution.* London: Cambridge University Press. Franklin, S. 1995. "Science as Culture, Cultures of Science." *Annual Review of Anthropology* 24:163–84. Marks, J. 2009. *Why I Am Not a Scientist: Anthropology and Modern Knowledge.* Berkeley: University of California Press.

7. Goldacre, B. 2009. *Bad Science.* London: Harper Perennial. Washington, H.A. 2012. *Deadly Monopolies.* New York: Random House. Kahn, J. 2012. *Race in a Bottle: The Story of BiDil and Racialized Medicine in a Post-Genomic Age.* New York: Columbia University Press.

8. Punnett, R.C. 1905. *Mendelism.* Cambridge: Macmillan and Bowes, p. 60.

9. Putnam, C. 1961. *Race and Reason.* Washington, DC: Public Affairs Press. Jackson, J.P., Jr. 2005. *Science for Segregation.* New York: NYU Press.

10. Dobzhansky, T. 1963. "Probability That *Homo sapiens* Evolved Independently 5 Times Is Vanishingly Small." *Current Anthropology* 4:360, 364–66. Birdsell, J. 1963. Review of *The Origin of Races,* by C.S. Coon. *Quarterly Review of Biology* 38:178–85. Garn, S. 1963. Review of *The Origin of Races,* by C.S. Coon. *American Sociological Review* 28:637–38. Caspari, R. 2003. "From Types to Populations: A Century of Race, Physical Anthropology, and the American Anthropological Association." *American Anthropologist* 105:65–76. Marks, J. 2008. "Race across the Physical-Cultural Divide in American Anthropology." In *A New History of Anthropology,* ed. H. Kuklick. New York: Wiley-Blackwell, pp. 242–58.

11. Dobzhansky, T. 1962. "Genetics and Equality." *Science* 137:112–15. Baker, L.D. 2010. *Anthropology and the Racial Politics of Culture.* Durham, NC: Duke University Press.

12. Cavalieri, P., and P. Singer, eds. 1993. *The Great Ape Project.* New York: St. Martin's Press.

13. Hunt-Grubbe, C. 2007. "The Elementary DNA of Dr. Watson." *Sunday Times London*, 14 October. Watson, J. 2007. *Avoid Boring People.* New York: Alfred A. Knopf.

14. Marks, J. 2009. "Is Poverty Better Explained by History of Colonialism?" *Nature* 458:145–46.

15. By "scientific racism" I mean the act of justifying social inequalities between groups of people by recourse to inferred natural difference, usually in terms of innate intellectual aptitudes. The most infamous example in recent memory was *The Bell Curve* (1994), by the psychologist Richard Herrnstein and the political theorist Charles Murray. More recent examples include *The 10,000 Year Explosion: How Civilization Accelerated Human Evolution* (2009), by the physicist Gregory Cochran and anthropologist Henry Harpending, and *A Troublesome Inheritance: Genes, Race and Human History* (2014), by the science journalist Nicholas Wade.

16. "From so simple a beginning endless forms most beautiful and most wonderful have been, and are being, evolved." Darwin, C. 1859. *On the Origin of Species by Means of Natural Selection, or the Preservation of Favoured Races in the Struggle for Life.* London: John Murray, p. 490. In this famous final sentence, Darwin intends not the modern sense of "differentiated" but the now-archaic sense of "developed" or "transmuted" from the simple to the complex. Unsurprisingly, the early decades of Darwinism commonly referred to it as "the development theory" or "transmutationism."

17. My discussion of the history of philosophy is necessarily attenuated. For extensive parsing of relativism, see Krausz, M. 2010. *Relativism: A Contemporary Anthropology.* New York: Columbia University Press.

18. Exodus 22:18; Galatians 5:20.

19. Lovejoy, A.O. 1936. *The Great Chain of Being.* Cambridge, MA: Harvard University Press.

20. Rousseau, J.-J. 1755. *Discours sur l'origine et les fondements de l'inégalité parmi les hommes.* Amsterdam: Marc Michel Rey.

21. Nisbet, R. 1980. *History of the Idea of Progress.* New York: Basic Books.

22. Benedict, R. 1934. *Patterns of Culture.* New York: Houghton Mifflin. They also drew on a European philosophical tradition that

included Wilhelm Dilthey, and increasingly began to root itself in anthropological data. Westermarck, E. 1932. *Ethical Relativity.* London: Kegan Paul, Trench, Trübner. The phrase "cultural relativity" appears for the first time in the *American Anthropologist* in 1939, and is not altered to "cultural relativism" until after World War II. Lesser, A. 1939. "Problems versus Subject Matter as Directives of Research." *American Anthropologist* 41:574–82. Williams, E. 1947. "Anthropology for the Common Man." *American Anthropologist* 49:84–90.

23. The Earl of Bridgewater commissioned a series of full-length scientific works in the 1830s that were intended to summarize the state of the natural sciences, whose facts were presumed to attest to the wisdom of creation. The treatises did not, however, age well, as the next generation saw them as little more than pietistic nonsense.

24. Radick, G. 2010. "Did Darwin Change His Mind about the Fuegians?" *Endeavour* 34:50–54. James, W. 2009. "Charles Darwin at the Cape." *Quest* 5:3–6. Desmond, A.J., and J.R. Moore. 2009. *Darwin's Sacred Cause: How a Hatred of Slavery Shaped Darwin's Views on Human Evolution.* New York: Houghton Mifflin Harcourt.

25. On the "American school" of craniology, see Hrdlička, A. 1918. "Physical Anthropology: Its Scope and Aims; Its History and Present Status in America." *American Journal of Physical Anthropology* 1:133–82. Stanton, W.R. 1960. *The Leopard's Spots: Scientific Attitudes toward Race in America, 1815–59.* Chicago: University of Chicago Press. Odom, H.H. 1967. "Generalizations of Race in Nineteenth-Century Physical Anthropology." *Isis* 58:5–18. Haller, J.S., Jr. 1970. "The Species Problem: Nineteenth-Century Concepts of Racial Inferiority in the Origin of Man Controversy." *American Anthropologist* 72:1319–29. Brace, C.L. 2005. *"Race" Is a Four-Letter Word: The Genesis of the Concept.* New York: Oxford University Press. Franz Boas was recruited as a physical anthropologist by Columbia earlier than Hrdlička, but did not concentrate on that area.

26. Cunningham, D. 1908. "Anthropology in the Eighteenth Century." *Journal of the Royal Anthropological Institute of Great Britain and Ireland* 38:10–35. Smith, G.E. 1935. "The Place of Thomas Henry Huxley in Anthropology." *Journal of the Royal Anthropological Institute of Great Britain and Ireland* 65:199–204. Stocking G.W. 1971. "What's in a Name?

The Origins of the Royal Anthropological Institute 1837–71." *Man* 63:369–90.

27. Zimmerman, A. 1999. "Anti-Semitism as Skill: Rudolf Virchow's *Schulstatistik* and the Racial Composition of Germany." *Central European History* 32:409–29. Manias, C. 2009. "The *Race prussienne* Controversy: Scientific Internationalism and the Nation." *Isis* 100:733–57.

28. Köpping, K. 1983. *Adolf Bastian and the Psychic Unity of Mankind.* St. Lucia: University of Queensland Press.

29. Spencer, F. 1979. "Aleš Hrdlička, MD, 1869–1943: A Chronicle of the Life and Work of an American Physical Anthropologist." PhD diss., University of Michigan. Marks, J. 2002. "Aleš Hrdlička." In *Celebrating a Century of the American Anthropological Association: Presidential Portraits,* ed. R. Darnell and F. Gleach. Arlington, VA: American Anthropological Association; Omaha: University of Nebraska Press, pp. 45–48.

30. Hooton, E. A. 1936. "Plain Statements about Race." *Science* 83:511–13. Barkan, E. A. 1993. *The Retreat of Scientific Racism.* New York: Cambridge University Press.

31. Anonymous. 1937. "'Biological Purge' Is Urged by Hooton. Harvard anthropologist says 'sit-down strike' in moron breeding is essential. Or unfit society will die. Howl of Roman mob for bread and circuses is re-echoing ominously, he declares." *New York Times,* 21 February. Hooton, E. A. 1939. *The American Criminal: An Anthropological Study.* Vol. 1, *The Native White Criminal of Native Parentage.* Cambridge, MA: Harvard University Press. Giles, E. 2012. "Two Faces of Earnest A. Hooton." *Yearbook of Physical Anthropology* 55:105–13.

32. Washburn, S. L. 1951. "The New Physical Anthropology." *Transactions of the New York Academy of Sciences, Series II,* 13:298–304.

33. Weiner, J. S. 1957. "Physical Anthropology: An Appraisal." *American Scientist* 45:79–87. Hulse, F. S. 1962. "Race as an Evolutionary Episode." *American Anthropologist* 64:929–45. Livingstone, F. B. 1962. "On the Non-existence of Human Races." *Current Anthropology* 3:279–81. Washburn, S. L. 1963. "The Study of Race." *American Anthropologist* 65:521–31.

34. Dupré, J. 1993. *The Disorder of Things: Metaphysical Foundations of the Disunity of Science.* Cambridge, MA: Harvard University Press.

35. Malinowski, B. 1935. *Coral Gardens and Their Magic.* London: Allen and Unwin.

36. Bacon, F. 1597. *Meditationes Sacrae*. London: Hooper.

37. Whewell, W. 1840. *The Philosophy of the Inductive Sciences*. London: John W. Parker.

38. Gregory, B. 2012. *The Unintended Reformation*. Cambridge, MA: Harvard University Press.

39. Strauss, D.F. 1835. *Das Leben Jesu kritisch bearbeitet*. Tübingen: C.F. Osiander.

CHAPTER TWO. HISTORY AND MORALITY

1. Numbers, R.L. 1992. *The Creationists*. New York: Knopf.

2. Harwit, M. 1996. *An Exhibit Denied: Lobbying the History of Enola Gay*. New York: Copernicus.

3. Anonymous. 2010. "Rewriting History in Texas." *New York Times* editorial, 15 March.

4. Darwin, C. 1866. *On the Origin of Species by Means of Natural Selection*. 4th ed. London: John Murray. Ruse, M. 1979. *The Darwinian Revolution: Nature Red in Tooth and Claw*. Chicago: University of Chicago Press. Eiseley, L. 1979. *Darwin and the Mysterious Mr. X*. New York: E.P. Dutton.

5. Mendel's role was to be adopted as a mythic ancestor for genetics. Bowler, P.J. 1989. *The Mendelian Revolution: The Emergence of Hereditarian Concepts in Modern Science and Society*. Baltimore: Johns Hopkins University Press.

6. Gleick, J. 2007. *Isaac Newton*. New York: Random House. Kohler, R.E. 1994. *Lords of the Fly: Drosophila Genetics and the Experimental Life*. Chicago: University of Chicago Press. Banner, L.W. 2010. *Intertwined Lives: Margaret Mead, Ruth Benedict, and Their Circle*. New York: Random House.

7. Lyell, C. 1830. *Principles of Geology*. Vol. 1. London: John Murray, p. 48.

8. Gordin, M.D. 2012. *The Pseudoscience Wars: Immanuel Velikovsky and the Birth of the Modern Fringe*. Chicago: University of Chicago Press.

9. Butterfield, H. [1931] 1965. *The Whig Interpretation of History*. New York: W.W. Norton.

10. Poole, W. 2010. *The World Makers: Scientists of the Restoration and the Search for the Origins of the Earth.* Oxford: Peter Lang.

11. Ray, J. 1691. *The Wisdom of God Manifested in the World Of Creation.* London: Samuel Smith. Gillespie, N. C. 1987. "Natural History, Natural Theology, and Social Order: John Ray and the 'Newtonian ideology.'" *Journal of the History of Biology* 20:1–49. Brooke, J. H. 1989. "Science and the Fortunes of Natural Theology: Some Historical Perspectives." *Zygon* 24:3–22. Gillespie, N. C. 1990. "Divine Design and the Industrial Revolution: William Paley's Abortive Reform of Natural Theology." *Isis* 81:214–29. Ospovat, D. 1995. *The Development Of Darwin's Theory: Natural History, Natural Theology, and Natural Selection, 1838–1859.* New York: Cambridge University Press. McGrath, A. E. 2013. *Darwinism and the Divine: Evolutionary Thought and Natural Theology.* New York: John Wiley & Sons.

12. Rudwick, M. J. 2005. *Bursting the Limits of Time: The Reconstruction of Geohistory in the Age of Revolution.* Chicago: University of Chicago Press.

13. Greene, J. C. 1954. "Some Early Speculations on the Origin of Human Races." *American Anthropologist* 56:31–41. Lurie, E. 1954. "Louis Agassiz and the Races of Man." *Isis* 45:227–42. Odom, H. H. 1967. "Generalizations of Race in Nineteenth-Century Physical Anthropology." *Isis* 58:5–18. Haller, J. S., Jr. 1970. "The Species Problem: Nineteenth-Century Concepts of Racial Inferiority in the Origin of Man Controversy." *American Anthropologist* 72:1319–29.

14. Van Riper, A. B. 1993. *Men among the Mammoths.* Chicago: University of Chicago Press. Livingstone, D. 2008. *Adam's Ancestors: Race, Religion, and the Politics of Human Origins.* Baltimore: Johns Hopkins University Press.

15. Trautmann, T. R. 1991. "The Revolution in Ethnological Time." *Man* 27:379–97. Augstein, H. F. 1997. "Linguistics and Politics in the Early 19th Century: James Cowles Prichard's Moral Philology." *History of European Ideas* 23:1–18. Benes, T. 2008. *In Babel's Shadow: Language, Philology, and the Nation in Nineteenth-Century Germany.* Detroit: Wayne State University Press. Browne, T. 2010. *The World Makers: Scientists of the Restoration and the Search for the Origins of the Earth.* Oxfordshire: Peter Lang.

16. López-Beltrán, C. 2004. "In the Cradle of Heredity; French Physicians and L'hérédité naturelle in the Early 19th Century." *Journal of the History of Biology* 37: 39–72. Müller-Wille, S., and H.-G. Rheinberger, eds. 2007. *Heredity Produced: At the Crossroads Of Biology, Politics, and Culture, 1500–1870*. Cambridge, MA: MIT Press. Müller-Wille, S., and H.-G. Rheinberger. 2012. *A Cultural History of Heredity*. Chicago: University of Chicago Press.

17. Plant cells and species on day three; animal cells and species on days five and six. The Bible makes no mention of microorganisms.

18. Livingstone, David N. 2014. *Dealing with Darwin: Place, Politics, and Rhetoric in Religious Engagements with Evolution*. Baltimore: Johns Hopkins University Press.

19. Haeckel, E. 1868. *Natürliche Schöpfungsgeschichte*. Berlin: Reimer. Kellogg, V. L. 1917. *Headquarters Nights: A Record of Conversations and Experiences at the Headquarters of the German Army in France and Belgium*. Boston: Atlantic Monthly Press.

20. Bryan, W.J. 1922. "God and Evolution." *New York Times*, 26 February.

21. As if they instinctively knew how to live there! This argument is often accompanied by the argument that all medical research on apes be stopped, despite the fact that diseases like Ebola are decimating the remaining wild ape populations.

22. Rupke, N. 2010. "Darwin's Choice." In *Biology and Ideology from Descartes to Dawkins*, ed. D. Alexander and R. L. Numbers. Chicago: University of Chicago Press, pp. 139–65. Bowler, P.J. 2013. *Darwin Deleted: Imagining a World without Darwin*. Chicago: University of Chicago Press.

23. Shaw, G. B. 1921. *Back to Methuselah: A Metabiological Pentateuch*. New York: Brentano's.

24. Haeckel, E. 1868. *Natürliche Schöpfungsgeschichte*. Berlin: Reimer. His grotesque racial caricatures appeared as the frontispiece of the first German edition, and were revised for the second German edition, but were omitted from the English translation. Marks, J. 2010. "Why Were the First Anthropologists Creationists?" *Evolutionary Anthropology* 19:222–26. Robert Chambers had suggested anonymously, in *Vestiges of the Natural History of Creation* (1844), that other races repre-

sented immature forms of Europeans, arrested at different stages in their development.

25. Richards, R. 2008. *The Tragic Sense of Life: Ernst Haeckel and the Struggle over Evolutionary Thought.* Chicago: University Of Chicago Press.

26. Eddy, J.H., Jr. 1984. "Buffon, Organic Alterations, and Man." *Studies in the History of Biology* 7:1–46.

27. The term came into wide use in the mid-twentieth century, as a retrospective label for a hodgepodge of late nineteenth-century works that tended to invoke Darwin as a justification for the avarice of the wealthy classes. Hofstadter, R. 1944. *Social Darwinism in American Thought.* Philadelphia: University of Pennsylvania Press. Hawkins, M. 1997. *Social Darwinism in European and American Thought, 1860–1945: Nature as Model and Nature as Threat.* New York: Cambridge University Press. Bannister, R. 2010. *Social Darwinism: Science and Myth in Anglo-American Social Thought.* Philadelphia: Temple University Press.

28. Pearl, R. 1927. "The Biology of Superiority." *American Mercury* 12:257–66. Muller, H.J. 1933. "The Dominance of Economics over Eugenics." *Scientific Monthly* 37:40–47. Allen, G.E. 1983. "The Misuse of Biological Hierarchies: The American Eugenics Movement, 1900–1940." *History and Philosophy of the Life Sciences* 5:105–28. Kevles, D.J. 1985. *In the Name of Eugenics.* Berkeley: University of California Press. Paul, D.B. 1995. *Controlling Human Heredity: 1865 to the Present.* Atlantic Highlands, NJ: Humanities Press International

29. Notably, physicist William Shockley, psychologist Henry Garrett, and anatomist Wesley Critz George. Jackson, J.P., Jr. 2005. *Science for Segregation.* New York: NYU Press.

30. Wilson, E.O. 1975. *Sociobiology: The New Synthesis.* Cambridge, MA: Harvard University Press. Dawkins, R. 1976. *The Selfish Gene.* Wade, N. 1976. "Sociobiology: Troubled Birth for New Discipline." *Science* 191:1151–55. Segerstråle, U.C.O. 2000. *Defenders of the Truth: The Battle for Science in the Sociobiology Debate and Beyond.* New York: Oxford University Press. Perez, M. 2013. "Evolutionary Activism: Stephen Jay Gould, the New Left and Sociobiology." *Endeavour* 37:104–11.

31. Zevit, Z. 2013. *What Really Happened in the Garden of Eden?* New Haven, CT: Yale University Press.

32. Hesiod, *Theogony* 520–25.

33. Kühl, S. 1994. *The Nazi Connection.* New York: Oxford University Press.

34. Lombardo, P. A. 2008. *Three Generations, No Imbeciles: Eugenics, the Supreme Court, and Buck v. Bell.* Baltimore: Johns Hopkins University Press.

35. Laughlin did not have a "real" doctorate, but was respected in the field. He published widely on genetics, including six papers on the subject in the *Proceedings of the National Academy of Sciences.*

36. Reverby, S. M. 2012. "Reflections on Apologies and the Studies in Tuskegee and Guatemala." *Ethics & Behavior* 22:493–95.

37. Skloot, R. 2010. *The Immortal Life of Henrietta Lacks.* New York: Crown.

38. Brigham, C. C. 1923. *A Study of American Intelligence.* Princeton, NJ: Princeton University Press. Herrnstein, R., and C. Murray. 1994. *The Bell Curve.* New York: Free Press.

39. Bolnick, D. A., et al. 2007. "The Science and Business of Genetic Ancestry Testing." *Science* 318:399–400. Nelson, A. 2008. "Bio Science: Genetic Genealogy Testing and the Pursuit of African Ancestry." *Social Studies of Science* 38:759–83. Murray, A. B. V., M. J. Carson, C. A. Morris, and J. Beckwith. 2010. "Illusions of Scientific Legitimacy: Misrepresented Science in the Direct-to-Consumer Genetic-Testing Marketplace." *Trends in Genetics* 26:459–61. Roberts, D. 2011. *Fatal Invention: How Science, Politics, and Big Business Re-Create Race in the Twenty-First Century.* New York: New Press. TallBear, K. 2013. *Native American DNA: Tribal Belonging and the False Promise of Genetic Science.* Minneapolis: University of Minnesota Press. Thomas, M. 2013. "To Claim Someone Has 'Viking Ancestors' Is No Better Than Astrology. *The Guardian UK,* 25 February, http://www.theguardian.com/science/blog/2013/feb/25/viking-ancestors-astrology.

40. Matthew 6:24; Luke 16:13.

CHAPTER THREE. EVOLUTIONARY CONCEPTS

1. Darwin, C. 1868. *The Variation of Animals and Plants under Domestication.* London: John Murray, p. 6.

2. Ogle, W. 1882. *Aristotle: On the Parts of Animals*. London: Kegan Paul, French.

3. Lachance, J., and S. A. Tishkoff. 2013. "Population Genomics of Human Adaptation." *Annual Review of Ecology, Evolution, and Systematics* 44:123–43.

4. Dean, G. 1971. *The Poryphyrias*. 2nd ed. Philadelphia: J.B. Lippincott.

5. Myrianthopoulos, N. C., and S. M. Aronson. 1966. "Population Dynamics of Tay-Sachs Disease I: Reproductive Fitness and Selection." *American Journal of Human Genetics* 18:313–27. Cochran, G., J. Hardy, and H. Harpending. 2005. "Natural History of Ashkenazi Intelligence." *Journal of Biosocial Science* 38:659–93.

6. Frisch, A., R. Colombo, E. Michaelovsky, M. Karpati, B. Goldman, and L. Peleg. 2004. "Origin and Spread of the 1278insTATC Mutation Causing Tay-Sachs Disease in Ashkenazi Jews: Genetic Drift as a Robust and Parsimonious Hypothesis." *Human Genetics* 114:366–76.

7. Valles, S. A. 2010. "The Mystery of the Mystery of Common Genetic Diseases." *Biology and Philosophy* 25:183–201.

8. Bobadilla, J. L., M. Macek, Jr., J. P. Fine, and P. M. Farrell, 2002. "Cystic Fibrosis: A Worldwide Analysis of CFTR Mutations—Correlation with Incidence Data and Application to Screening." *Human Mutation* 19:575–606.

9. Jacob, F. 1977. "Evolution and Tinkering." *Science* 196:1161–66.

10. Morgan, T. H. 1913. "Factors and Unit Characters in Mendelian Heredity." *American Naturalist* 47:5–16. Castle, W. E. 1930. "Race Mixture and Physical Disharmonies." *Science* 71:603–6. Gates, R. R. 1934. "The Unit Character in Genetics." *Nature* 133:138.

11. This tension was visible a century ago. Gregory, W. 1917. "Genetics versus Paleontology." *American Naturalist* 51:622–35.

12. Sarich, V., and A. Wilson. 1967a. "Rates of Albumin Evolution in Primates." *Proceedings of the National Academy of Sciences of the United States of America* 58:142–48. Sarich, V., and A. Wilson. 1967b. "Immunological Time Scale for Hominid Evolution." *Science* 158:1200-1203.

13. Enard, W., M. Przeworski, S. E. Fisher, C. S. Lai, V. Wiebe, T. Kitano, A. P. Monaco, and S. Pääbo. 2002. "Molecular Evolution of

FOXP2, a Gene Involved in Speech and Language." *Nature* 418:869–72. Fisher, S.E., and C. Scharff. 2009. "FOXP2 as a Molecular Window into Speech and Language." *Trends in Genetics* 25:166–77.

14. Myers, R.H., and D.A. Shafer. 1979. "Hybrid Ape Offspring of a Mating of Gibbon and Siamang." *Science* 205:308–10. Godfrey, L., and J. Marks. 1991. "The Nature and Origins of Primate Species." *Yearbook of Physical Anthropology* 34:39–68.

15. Hooton, E.A. 1930. "Doubts and Suspicions Concerning Certain Functional Theories of Primate Evolution." *Human Biology* 2:223–49. Washburn, S.L. 1963. "The Study of Race." *American Anthropologist* 65:521–31. Gould, S.J., and R.C. Lewontin. 1979. "The Spandrels of San Marco and the Panglossian Paradigm: A Critique of the Adaptationist Programme." *Proceedings of the Royal Society of London, Series B,* 205:581–98.

16. Gould, S.J. 1997. "Darwinian Fundamentalism." *New York Review of Books,* 12 June, 34–37.

17. Dawkins, R. 1976. *The Selfish Gene.* New York: Oxford University Press, p. 19.

18. Simpson, G.G. 1951. "The Species Concept." *Evolution* 5:285–98. Hausdorf, B. 2011. "Progress toward a General Species Concept." *Evolution* 65:923–31. Sloan, P.R. 2013. "The Species Problem and History." *Studies in History and Philosophy of Biology and Biomedical Science* 44:237–41.

19. Paterson, H.E.H. 1985. "The Recognition Concept of Species." In *Species and Speciation,* ed. E.S. Vrba. Pretoria: Transvaal Museum, pp. 21–29. Mendelson, T.C., and K.L. Shaw. 2012. "The (Mis)concept of Species Recognition." *Trends in Ecology and Evolution* 27:421–27.

20. Dobzhansky, T. 1937. *Genetics and the Origin of Species.* New York: Columbia University Press. Mayr, E. 1942. *Systematics and the Origin of Species.* New York: Columbia University Press.

21. Dobzhansky, T., F. Ayala, G. Stebbins, and J. Valentine. 1977. *Evolution.* San Francisco: W.H. Freeman. Mayr, E. 1988. *Toward a New Philosophy of Biology: Observations of an Evolutionist.* Cambridge, MA: Harvard University Press.

22. Waddington, C.H. 1938. *An Introduction to Modern Genetics.* London: George Allen and Unwin.

23. Novikoff, A. 1945. "The Concept of Integrative Levels and Biology." *Science* 101:209–15.

24. Marks, J. 2005. "Phylogenetic Trees and Evolutionary Forests." *Evolutionary Anthropology* 14:49–53. Marks, J. 2007. "Anthropological Taxonomy as Both Subject and Object: The Consequences of Descent from Darwin and Durkheim." *Anthropology Today* 23:7–12.

25. Raup, D.M. 1994. "The Role of Extinction in Evolution." *Proceedings of the National Academy of Sciences* 91:6758–63. Gould, S.J. 2003. *The Structure of Evolutionary Theory.* Cambridge, MA: Harvard University Press.

26. Morris, S.C. 2003. *Life's Solution: Inevitable Humans in a Lonely Universe.* New York: Cambridge University Press.

27. Simpson, G.G. 1964. "The Nonprevalence of Humanoids." *Science* 143:769–75.

28. Eldredge, N., and S.J. Gould. 1972. "Punctuated Equilibria: An Alternative to Phyletic Gradualism." In *Models in Paleobiology,* ed. T.J. Schopf. San Francisco: W.H. Freeman, pp. 82–115. Gould, S.J., and N. Eldredge. 1977. "Punctuated Equilibria: The Tempo and Mode of Evolution Reconsidered." *Paleobiology,* 115–51.

29. Tattersall, I., and N. Eldredge. 1977. "Fact, Theory, and Fantasy in Human Paleontology." *American Scientist* 65:204–11.

30. Kottler, M.J. 1974. "From 48 to 46: Cytological Technique, Preconception, and the Counting of Human Chromosomes." *Bulletin of the History of Medicine* 48:475–502. Martin, A. 2004. "Can't Any Body Count? Counting as an Epistemic Theme in the History of Human Chromosomes." *Social Studies of Science* 34:923–48. Gartler, S.M. 2006. "The Chromosome Number in Humans: A Brief History." *Nature Reviews Genetics* 7:655–60.

31. Landau, M. 1991. *Narratives of Human Evolution.* New Haven, CT: Yale University Press. Sussman, R.W. 1999. "The Myth of Man the Hunter, Man the Killer and the Evolution of Human Morality." *Zygon* 34:453–71. Stoczkowski, W. 2002. *Explaining Human Origins: Myth, Imagination and Conjecture.* New York: Cambridge University Press. Pyne, L.V., and S.J. Pyne. 2012. *The Last Lost World: Ice Ages, Human Origins, and the Invention of the Pleistocene.* New York: Penguin.

32. Kirk Douglas was formerly Isidore Demsky, and Ashley Montagu was formerly Israel Ehrenberg. The pianist Olga Samaroff renamed

herself to sound more, and differently, ethnic; the journalist Henry Morton Stanley renamed himself to conceal his humble origins.

33. Candida Moss kindly points out that although both genealogies pass through David, their aims are slightly divergent. Matthew's goal is to connect Jesus to Abraham, while Luke's goal is to connect Jesus to Adam.

34. http://www.rootsforreal.com/dna_en.php.

35. Skorecki, K., S. Selig, S. Blazer, R. Bradman, N. Bradman, P.J. Warburton, M. Ismjlowicz, and M.F. Hammer. 1997. "Y Chromosomes of Jewish Priests." *Nature* 385:32. M.G. Thomas, K. Skorecki, H. Ben-Ami, T. Parfitt, N. Bradman, and D. Goldstein. 1998. "Origins of Old Testament Priests." *Nature* 394:138–39. M.G.Thomas, T. Parfitt, D.A. Weiss, K. Skorecki, J. Wilson, M. le Roux, N. Bradman, and D. Goldstein. 2000. "Y Chromosomes Traveling South: The Cohen Modal Haplotype and the Origins of the Lemba—the 'Black Jews of Southern Africa.'" *American Journal of Human Genetics* 66:674–86. Zoossmann-Diskin, A. 2000. "Are Today's Jewish Priests Descended from the Old Ones?" *Homo* 51:156–62. H. Soodyall. 2013. "Lemba Origins Revisited: Tracing the Ancestry of Y Chromosomes in South African and Zimbabwean Lemba." *South African Medical Journal* 103:1009–13. Marks, J. 2013. "The Nature/Culture of Genetic Facts." *Annual Review of Anthropology* 42:247–67.

36. Nelkin, D., and M. Susan Lindee. 1995. *The DNA Mystique: The Gene as Cultural Icon.* New York: Freeman. El-Haj, N.A. 2012. *The Genealogical Science: The Search for Jewish Origins and the Politics of Epistemology.* Chicago: University of Chicago Press. Jobling, M.A. 2012. "The Impact of Recent Events on Human Genetic Diversity." *Philosophical Transactions of the Royal Society B: Biological Sciences* 367:793–99.

37. Lima, M. 2014. *The Book of Trees.* New York: Princeton Architectural Press.

38. http://hsblogs.stanford.edu/morrison/2011/03/10/human-genome-diversity-project-frequently-asked-questions/.

39. Lordkipanidze, D., M.S.P. de León, A. Margvelashvili, Y. Rak, G.P. Rightmire, A. Vekua, and C.P. Zollikofer. 2013. "A Complete Skull from Dmanisi, Georgia, and the Evolutionary Biology of Early *Homo.*" *Science* 342:326–31.

40. Hooton, E.A. 1931; 1946. *Up from the Ape.* New York: Macmillan. Weidenreich, F. 1947. "Facts and Speculations Concerning the Origin of *Homo sapiens*." *American Anthropologist* 49:187–203. Hulse, F.S. 1962. "Race as an Evolutionary Episode." *American Anthropologist* 64:929–45. Wolpoff, M.H., and R. Caspari. 1997. *Race and Human Evolution.* New York: Simon and Schuster.

CHAPTER FOUR. HOW TO THINK ABOUT
EVOLUTION NON-REDUCTIVELY

1. Mayr, E. 1959. "Where Are We?" *Cold Spring Harbor Symposium in Quantitative Biology* 24:1–14. Rao, V., and V. Nanjundiah. 2011. "J.B.S. Haldane, Ernst Mayr and the Beanbag Genetics Dispute." *Journal of the History of Biology* 44:233–81.

2. Lewontin, R.C. 1970. "The Units of Selection." *Annual Review of Ecology and Systematics* 1:1–18. Gould, S.J. 1980. "Is a New and General Theory of Evolution Emerging?" *Paleobiology* 6:119–30. Eldredge, N. 1985. *Unfinished Synthesis: Biological Hierarchies and Modern Evolutionary Thought.* New York: Oxford University Press.

3. In a bit of a twist, a recent debate about evolutionary theory in *Nature* had conservative biologists invoking Waddington paradoxically in defense of their own normative reductionism. Laland, K., T. Uller, M. Feldman, K. Sterelny, G.B. Müller, A. Moczek, E. Jablonka, J. Odling-Smee, G.A. Wray, H.E. Hoekstra, D.J. Futuyma, R.E. Lenski, T.F.C. Mackay, D. Schluter, and J.E. Strassmann. 2014. "Does Evolutionary Theory Need a Rethink?" *Nature* 514:161–64.

4. Waddington, C.H. 1959. "Evolutionary Systems—Animal and Human." *Nature* 183:1634–38.

5. Waddington, C.H. 1975. *The Evolution of an Evolutionist.* Ithaca, NY: Cornell University Press, p. 5.

6. Doolittle, W.F. 2013. "Is Junk DNA Bunk? A Critique of ENCODE." *Proceedings of the National Academy of Sciences* 110:5294–5300.

7. King, J.L., and T.H. Jukes. 1969. "Non-Darwinian Evolution." *Science* 164:788–98.

8. Lévi-Strauss, C. 1962. *The Savage Mind*. Chicago: University of Chicago Press. Jacob, F. 1977. "Evolution and Tinkering." *Science* 196:1161–66.

9. Carbone, L., et al. 2014. "Gibbon Genome and the Fast Karyotype Evolution of Small Apes." *Nature* 513:195–201.

10. Waddington, C.H. 1957. *The Strategy of the Genes*. London: Allen and Unwin.

11. West-Eberhard, M.J. 2003. *Developmental Plasticity and Evolution*. New York: Oxford University Press.

12. Waddington, C.H. 1956. "Genetic Assimilation of the Bithorax Phenotype." *Evolution* 10:1–13.

13. Marks, J. 1989. "Genetic Assimilation in the Evolution of Bipedalism." *Human Evolution* 4:493–99.

14. Standen, E.M., T.Y. Du, and H.C.E. Larsson. 2014. "Developmental Plasticity and the Origin of Tetrapods." *Nature* 513:54–58.

15. "[Caliban is] A devil, a born devil, on whose nature / Nurture can never stick, on whom my pains / Humanely taken, all, all lost, quite lost." *The Tempest*, act 4, scene 1.

16. Jones, L.A. 1923. "Would Direct Evolution." *New York Times*, 2 December.

17. Koestler, A. 1972. *The Case of the Midwife Toad*. New York: Random House. Gliboff, S. 2005. "'Protoplasm ... Is Soft Wax in Our Hands': Paul Kammerer and the Art of Biological Transformation." *Endeavour* 29:162–67. Gliboff, S. 2006. "The Case of Paul Kammerer: Evolution and Experimentation in the Early 20th Century." *Journal of the History of Biology* 39:525–63.

18. Sinnott, E.W., and L.C. Dunn. 1925. *Principles of Genetics*. New York: McGraw-Hill, p. 406.

19. James D. Watson, quoted in Jaroff, L. 1989. "The Gene Hunt." *Time*, 20 March, p. 67.

20. Fuentes, A. 2004. "It's Not All Sex and Violence: Integrated Anthropology and the Role of Cooperation and Social Complexity in Human Evolution." *American Anthropologist* 106:710–18. Laland, K.N., and M.J. O'Brien. 2011. "Cultural Niche Construction: An Introduction." *Biological Theory* 6:191–202. Kendal, J.R. 2011. "Cultural Niche Construction and Human Learning Environments: Investigating

Sociocultural Perspectives." *Biological Theory* 6:241–50. Sterelny, K. 2012. *The Evolved Apprentice.* Cambridge, MA: MIT Press. Fuentes, A. 2013. "Cooperation, Conflict, and Niche Construction in the Genus *Homo.*" In *War, Peace, and Human Nature,* ed. D. Fry. New York: Oxford University Press, pp. 78–94.

21. Kivell, T. L., J. M. Kibii, S. E. Churchill, P. Schmid, and L. R. Berger. 2011. "*Australopithecus sediba* Hand Demonstrates Mosaic Evolution of Locomotor and Manipulative Abilities." *Science* 333:1411–17.

22. Wrangham, R. 2009. *Catching Fire.* Cambridge, MA: Harvard University Press. Burton, F. D. 2011. *Fire: The Spark That Ignited Human Evolution.* Albuquerque: University of New Mexico Press.

23. Horan, R. D., E. Bulte, and J. F. Shogren. 2005. "How Trade Saved Humanity from Biological Exclusion: An Economic Theory of Neanderthal Extinction." *Journal of Economic Behavior & Organization* 58:1–29. Oka, R., and A. Fuentes. 2010. "From Reciprocity to Trade: How Cooperative Infrastructures Form the Basis of Human Socioeconomic Evolution." In *Cooperation in Economy and Society,* ed. R. Marshall. Lanham, MD: AltaMira Press, pp. 3–27.

24. Graeber, D. 2011. *Debt: The First 5,000 Years.* New York: Melville House.

25. Kropotkin, P. 1916. *Mutual Aid.* New York: Knopf.

26. Giacobini, G 2007. "Richness and Diversity of Burial Rituals in the Upper Paleolithic." *Diogenes* 54:19–39.

27. Kluckhohn, C. 1949. *Mirror for Man.* New York: McGraw-Hill, p. 17.

28. Modified from the discussion in Hauser, M. D. 2009. "The Possibility of Impossible Cultures." *Nature* 460:190–96.

29. Suddendorf, T. 2013. *The Gap: The Science of What Separates Us from Other Animals.* New York: Basic Books. Some domestic animals have been bred to be responsive to human cues, and can consequently recognize pointing.

30. "An implication of the 'Machiavellian Intelligence' theory is that it was humans' increasingly sophisticated capacity for deceiving one another which eventually gave rise to that entirely novel level of representational activity which we call 'symbolic culture'." Knight, C., R. Dunbar, and C. Power 1999. "An Evolutionary Approach to Human

Culture." In *The Evolution of Culture,* ed. R. Dunbar, C. Knight, and C. Power. New York: Routledge, p. 6.

31. Hobbes, T. 1651. *Leviathan or The Matter, Forme and Power of a Common Wealth Ecclesiasticall and Civil.* Vico, G. 1725. *Principi di scienza nuova d'intorno alla comune natura delle nazioni.*

32. Arcadi, A.C. 2000. "Vocal Responsiveness in Male Wild Chimpanzees: Implications for the Evolution of Language." *Journal of Human Evolution* 39:205–23.

33. Leach, E.R. 1958. "Magical Hair." *Journal of the Anthropological Institute of Great Britain and Ireland* 88:147–64. Hallpike, C.R. 1969. "Social Hair." *Man* 4:256–64. Berman, J.C. 1999. "Bad Hair Days in the Paleolithic: Modern (Re)Constructions of the Cave Man." *American Anthropologist* 101:288–304.

34. Childe, V.G. 1936. *Man Makes Himself.* London: Watts. White, L.A. 1959. *The Evolution of Culture.* New York: McGraw-Hill.

35. Sterelny, K. 2001. *Dawkins vs. Gould: Survival of the Fittest.* Cambridge: Icon Books/Totem Books. Gould, S.J. 2003. *The Structure of Evolutionary Theory.* Cambridge, MA: Harvard University Press. Pigliucci, M. 2009. "An Extended Synthesis for Evolutionary Biology." *Annals of the New York Academy of Sciences* 1168:218–28.

36. Simpson, G.G. 1953. *The Major Features of Evolution.* New York: Columbia University Press.

37. One genome won't work presumably because harmful recessive mutations would invariably be expressed in a haploid organism. But that doesn't explain why three genomes won't work either.

38. Ayala, F.J. 2010. "The Difference of Being Human: Morality." *Proceedings of the National Academy of Sciences, USA,* 107:9020; emphasis in original.

CHAPTER FIVE. HOW OUR ANCESTORS TRANSGRESSED THE BOUNDARIES OF APEHOOD

1. "Les Anglois ne sont pas réduits comme nous à un seul nom pour désigner les singes; ils ont, comme les Grecs, deux noms différens, l'un pour les singes sans queue qu'ils appellent ape, et l'autre pour les

singes à queue qu'ils appellent monkie." Comte de Buffon. 1749. *Histoire naturelle, générale et particulière.* Vol. 14. Paris: Imprimerie Royale, pp. 66–67.

2. Van Wyhe, J. 2005. "The Descent of Words: Evolutionary Thinking 1780–1880." *Endeavour* 29:94–100.

3. Huxley, T.H. 1863. *Evidence as to Man's Place in Nature.* New York. D. Appleton, p. 130.

4. Simpson, G.G. 1949. *The Meaning of Evolution.* New Haven, CT: Yale University Press, p. 283.

5. Morris, D. 1967. *The Naked Ape.* New York: McGraw-Hill. Diamond, J. 1992. *The Third Chimpanzee.* New York: HarperCollins. Coyne, J. 2010. *Why Evolution Is True.* New York: Viking.

6. Goodman, M. 1963. "Man's Place in the Phylogeny of the Primates as Reflected in Serum Proteins." In *Classification and Human Evolution,* ed. S.L. Washburn. Chicago: Aldine, pp. 204–34. Sommer, M. 2008. "History in the Gene: Negotiations between Molecular and Organismal Anthropology." *Journal of the History of Biology* 41:473–528. Hagen, J.B. 2009. "Descended from Darwin? George Gaylord Simpson, Morris Goodman, and Primate Systematics." In *Descended from Darwin: Insights into the History of Evolutionary Studies, 1900–1970,* ed. J. Cain and M. Ruse. Philadelphia: American Philosophical Society, pp. 93–109. Marks, J. 2009. "What Is the Viewpoint of Hemoglobin, and Does It Matter?" *History and Philosophy of the Life Sciences* 31:239–60.

7. Marks, J. 2002. *What It Means to Be 98% Chimpanzee.* Berkeley: University of California Press.

8. Shubin, N. 2009. *Your Inner Fish: A Journey into the 3.5-Billion-Year History of the Human Body.* New York: Vintage.

9. Wildman, D.E., M. Uddin, G. Liu, L.I. Grossman, and M. Goodman. 2003. "Implications of Natural Selection in Shaping 99.4% Nonsynonymous DNA Identity between Humans and Chimpanzees: Enlarging Genus *Homo.*" *Proceedings of the National Academy of Sciences, USA,* 100:7181–88.

10. Cuvier, G. 1817. *Le regne animal distribué d'après son organisation, pour servir de base a l'histoire naturelle des animaux.* Paris: Deterville.

11. Gregory, W.K. 1910. "The Orders of Mammals." *Bulletin of the American Museum of Natural History* 27. Simpson, G.G. 1945. "The Prin-

ciples of Classification and a Classification of Mammals." *Bulletin of the American Museum of Natural History* 85.

12. Groves, C. 2001. *Primate Taxonomy.* Washington, DC: Smithsonian Institution Press.

13. Sawyer, G., and V. Deak. 2007. *The Last Human: A Guide to Twenty-Two Species of Extinct Humans.* New Haven, CT: Yale University Press. White, T.D. 2008. Review of *The Last Human: A Guide to Twenty-Two Species of Extinct Humans,* by G.J. Sawyer and Viktor Deak. *Quarterly Review of Biology* 83:105–6.

14. Rylands, A.B., and R.A. Mittermeier. 2014. "Primate Taxonomy: Species and Conservation." *Evolutionary Anthropology* 23:8–10.

15. Simpson 1945, 188.

16. Langdon, J.H. 2005. *The Human Strategy: An Evolutionary Perspective on Human Anatomy.* New York: Oxford University Press.

17. Zipfel, B., J.M. DeSilva, R.S. Kidd, K.J. Carlson, S.E. Churchill, and L.R. Berger. 2011. "The Foot and Ankle of *Australopithecus sediba*." *Science* 333:1417–20. Haile-Selassie, Y., B.Z. Saylor, A. Deino, N.E. Levin, M. Alene, and B.M. Latimer. 2012. "A New Hominin Foot from Ethiopia Shows Multiple Pliocene Bipedal Adaptations." *Nature* 483:565–69.

18. Bramble, D.M., and D.E. Lieberman. 2004. "Endurance Running and the Evolution of *Homo.*" *Nature* 432:345–52.

19. The continuity can be seen by comparing the South African cranial material assigned to *Australopithecus,* notably, STS-5 from Sterkfontein and MH-1 from Malapa, with South African *Paranthropus,* such as DNH-7 from Drimolen, and early *Homo,* such as Stw-53 from Sterkfontein and ER-1813 from Kenya.

20. Antón, S.C., R. Potts, and L.C. Aiello. 2014. "Evolution of Early *Homo:* An Integrated Biological Perspective." *Science* 345:45.

21. James VanderKam kindly tells me that the non-canonical Book of Jubilees (3:27) has Adam burning some incense as an offering to God, which presumes that the first man had figured it out.

22. Combe, G. 1854. *Lectures on Phrenology.* 3rd ed. New York: Fowlers and Wells. Davies, J.D. 1955. *Phrenology, Fad and Science: A 19th-Century American Crusade.* New Haven, CT: Yale University Press.

23. There are still a few psychologists who maintain this. Actually, however, the correlation of IQ with brain size is far lower than the cor-

relation of brain size with body size. In other words, big people tend to have big brains. If it were true that brain size were a significant determinant of intelligence, then the smartest people on earth would be football linemen.

24. Gould, S.J. 1981. *The Mismeasure of Man.* New York: W.W. Norton.

25. Boas, F. 1912. "Changes in the Bodily Form of Descendants of Immigrants." *American Anthropologist* 14:530–62.

26. Hrdlička, A. 1901. "An Eskimo Brain." *American Anthropologist* 3:454–500. This was the brain of Qisuk, one of the "New York Eskimos" whom Franz Boas convinced Robert Peary to bring to the Big Apple from the Arctic. All but Qisuk's son died within a few months. I discussed this in chapter 8 of *Why I Am Not a Scientist.*

27. Marks, J. 2010. "The Two 20th Century Crises of Racial Anthropology." In *Histories of American Physical Anthropology in the Twentieth Century,* ed. M.A. Little, and K.A.R. Kennedy. Lanham, MD: Lexington Books, pp. 187–206.

28. Washburn, S.L. 1951. "The New Physical Anthropology." *Transactions of the New York Academy of Sciences, Series II,* 13:298–304.

29. Bonogofsky, M. 2011. *The Bioarchaeology of the Human Head: Decapitation, Decoration, and Deformation.* Gainesville: University Press of Florida.

30. Krogman, W.M. 1951. "The Scars of Human Evolution." *Scientific American* 185 (December): 54–57.

31. Deacon, T. 1997. *The Symbolic Species.* New York: Norton.

32. http://atlantablackstar.com/2012/10/29/dominican-republic-continues-racist-treatment-of-haitians-75-years-after-massacre/. A more recent story had Lebanese militias differentiating between the Lebanese and Palestinian pronunciations of the Arabic word for "tomato." http://thenewinquiry.com/blogs/southsouth/pronunciation-as-death-sentence/.

33. There are other anatomical features as well, which are often not very successful without another person around, such as having the baby rotate in the birth canal, so that it emerges facing a different way than an ape baby does. Trevathan, W. 1987. *Human Birth: An Evolutionary Perspective.* Piscataway, NJ: Aldine Transaction. Rosenberg, K.R. 1992.

"The Evolution of Modern Human Childbirth." *Yearbook of Physical Anthropology* 35:89–124. Trevathan, W., and K.R. Rosenberg. 2000. "The Shoulders Follow the Head: Postcranial Constraints on Human Childbirth." *Journal of Human Evolution* 39:583–86.

34. Maclarnon, A., and G. Hewitt. 2004. "Increased Breathing Control: Another Factor in the Evolution of Human Language." *Evolutionary Anthropology* 13:181–97.

35. Sapir, E. 1921. *Language: An Introduction to the Study of Speech.* New York: Harcourt, Brace.

CHAPTER SIX. HUMAN EVOLUTION AS BIO-CULTURAL EVOLUTION

1. Westermarck, E. 1906. *The Origin and Development of the Moral Ideas.* London: Macmillan. Gayon, J. 2006. "Are There Metaphysical Implications of Darwinian Evolutionary Biology?" In *Darwinism and Philosophy,* ed. Vittorio Hösle and Christian Illies. Notre Dame, IN: University of Notre Dame Press, pp. 181–95.

2. The truth of this statement may be more literary than literal, given the epistemological problem associated with not being able to know what another species is actually thinking. The issue does generate a lot of heat. Some biologically sophisticated theologians have begun to grapple with the primate phylogenetic context of moral questions. Celia Deane-Drummond seeks to identify a middle ground of "intermorality" between those who insist that apes, say, are fully moral actors, like people, and those who insist that humans are literally completely different. Deane-Drummond, C. 2014. *The Wisdom of the Liminal: Human Nature, Evolution, and Other Animals.* Grand Rapids, MI: Eerdmans. Likewise, Wentzel van Huyssteen explores the meaning of human existence in a post-Darwinian universe in van Huyssteen, J. W. 2006. *Alone in the World? Human Uniqueness in Science and Theology.* Grand Rapids, MI: Eerdmans. See also Peters, K.E. 2007. "Toward an Evolutionary Christian Theology." *Zygon* 42:49–64; and McGrath, A. 2011. *Darwinism and the Divine.* New York: Wiley-Blackwell.

3. Although the curse has also traditionally been taken to include painful parturition, which is certainly a part of the human condition,

the curse on Eve is more likely about making her responsible for procreation itself. See Meyers, C. 2013. *Rediscovering Eve: Ancient Israelite Women in Context.* New York: Oxford University Press; Baden, J., and C.R. Moss. 2015. *Reconceiving Infertility.* Princeton, NJ: Princeton University Press.

4. Genesis 2 is about "the Lord God" making people, and Genesis 3 is about "God" introducing rule-governed behavior into human life. Another popular way of understanding the story is to follow Saint Augustine, and introduce Satan and original sin into the story, but that is not a literal reading, and is thus not germane to the discussion of what the story actually says.

5. This is of course *not* the origin of the Jewish prohibition on ham, which comes in Leviticus 11:7. The devil made me say that.

6. The Talmud suggests that Ham may have sodomized or even castrated Noah. Babylonian Talmud Sanhedrin 70a. Simply looking at another person's genitalia may have been nearly tantamount to raping them in the ancient Near East, and raping your father visually would be a sign of considerable disrespect to your parent. The text is so weird that Genesis 9:24 specifies that the crime was committed by the youngest son, Ham, whose son is cursed on his account, but Genesis 6:10 and 7:13 imply that Japheth was the youngest. Whatever the "original" story may have said, those Bronze Age shepherds clearly were really into patriarchy, and hated the Canaanites. Goldenberg, D. 2005. "What Did Ham Do to Noah?" In *"The Words of a Wise Man's Mouth Are Gracious," QOH 10,12: Festschrift for Günter Stemberger on the Occasion of His 65th Birthday,* ed. M. Perani. Berlin: Walter de Gruyter, pp. 257–65. Driver, S.R. 1916. *The Book of Genesis.* 10th ed. London: Methuen.

7. Other rivals, the Edomites, were ostensibly descended from Esau, who voluntarily surrendered his claim to the land of his brother Israel one day because he was really, really hungry.

8. Kuper, A. 2002. "Incest, Cousin Marriage, and the Origin of the Human Sciences in Nineteenth-Century England." *Present and Past* 174:158–83. Bittles, A.H., and M.L. Black. 2010. "Consanguineous Marriage and Human Evolution." *Annual Review of Anthropology* 39:193–207.

9. http://celebritybabies.people.com/2012/03/23/mad-men-january-jones-placenta-capsules-not-witch-crafty/.

10. The most famous example is brain consumption in New Guinea, which was found to be facilitating the transmission of a disease called kuru, and led to the discovery of prions. Lindenbaum, S. 2001. "Kuru, Prions, and Human Affairs: Thinking about Epidemics." *Annual Review of Anthropology* 30:363–85. Anderson, W. 2008. *The Collectors of Lost Souls: Turning Kuru Scientists into Whitemen.* Baltimore: Johns Hopkins University Press.

11. *Iliad,* book 22.

12. Cannabalism in non-starvation situations is no less powerfully symbolic for being well documented ethnographically. It is generally associated with special situations—such as war, mourning, or illness—and is generally magically charged, unlike consuming ordinary food. Consequently, practitioners of "corpse medicine" in the seventeenth century took considerable rhetorical pains to distinguish their cannibalistic treatments from cannibalism. Conklin, B. 2001. *Consuming Grief: Compassionate Cannibalism in an Amazonian Society.* Austin: University of Texas Press. Sugg, R. 2011. *Mummies, Cannibals, and Vampires: The History of Corpse Medicine from the Renaissance to the Victorians.* New York: Routledge.

13. Leviticus 20:11–21.

14. Arens, W. 1986. *The Original Sin: Incest and Its Meaning.* New York: Oxford University Press. Spain, D.H. 1987. "The Westermarck-Freud Incest-Theory Debate: An Evaluation and Reformulation." *Current Anthropology* 28:623–45.

15. Wolf, A.P. 1966. "Childhood Association, Sexual Attraction, and the Incest Taboo: A Chinese Case." *American Anthropologist* 68:883–98. Shepher, J. 1971. "Mate Selection among Second Generation Kibbutz Adolescents and Adults: Incest Avoidance and Negative Imprinting." *Archives of Sexual Behavior* 1:293–307. Leavitt, G.C. 1990. "Sociobiological Explanations of Incest Avoidance: A Critical Review of Evidential Claims." *American Anthropologist* 92:971–93. Shor, E., and D. Simchai. 2009. "Incest Avoidance, the Incest Taboo, and Social Cohesion: Revisiting Westermarck and the Case of the Israeli Kibbutzim." *American Journal of Sociology* 114:1803–42.

16. White, L.A. 1948. "The Definition and Prohibition of Incest." *American Anthropologist* 50:416–35. Parker, S. 1976. "The Precultural Basis

of the Incest Taboo: Toward a Biosocial Theory." *American Anthropologist* 78:285–305.

17. Hopkins, K. 1980. "Brother-Sister Marriage in Roman Egypt." *Comparative Studies in Society and History* 22:303–54. Shaw, B. D. 1992. "Explaining Incest: Brother-Sister Marriage in Graeco-Roman Egypt." *Man* 27:267–99. Parker, S. 1996. "Full Brother Sister Marriage in Roman Egypt: Another Look." *Cultural Anthropology* 11:362–76.

18. Strier, K. 2004. "Sociality among Kin and Nonkin in Nonhuman Primate Groups." In *The Origins and Nature of Sociality*, ed. R W. Sussman and A. R. Chapman. New York: Aldine/Transaction, pp. 191–214. Chapais, B. 2008. *Primeval Kinship*. Cambridge, MA: Harvard University Press.

19. Bogin, B. 1988. *Patterns of Human Growth*. New York: Cambridge University Press.

20. Diamond, J. 1992. *The Third Chimpanzee*. New York: HarperCollins. Klein, R. 2009. *The Human Career*. 3rd ed. Chicago: University of Chicago Press.

21. McBrearty, S., and A. S. Brooks. 2000. "The Revolution That Wasn't: A New Interpretation of the Origin of Modern Human Behavior." *Journal of Human Evolution* 39:453–563. Gamble, C. S. 2007. *Origins and Revolutions: Human Identity in Earliest Prehistory*. New York: Cambridge University Press. Shea, J. J. 2011. "*Homo sapiens* Is as *Homo sapiens* Was: Behavioral Variability versus 'Behavioral Modernity' in Paleolithic Archaeology." *Current Anthropology* 52:1–35. Caspari, R., and M. Wolpoff. 2013. "The Process of Modern Human Origins: The Evolutionary and Demographic Changes Giving Rise to Modern Humans." In *The Origins of Modern Humans: Biology Reconsidered*, ed. F. H. Smith and C. M. Ahern. New York: John Wiley & Sons.

22. Lévi-Strauss, C. 1969. *The Elementary Structures of Kinship*. Boston: Beacon Press, p. 24.

23. Aberle, D. F., U. Bronfenbrenner, E. H. Hess, D. R. Miller, D. M. Schneider, et al. 1963. "The Incest Taboo and the Mating Patterns of Animals." *American Anthropologist* 65:253–65.

24. Pickering, T. R. 2013. *Rough and Tumble: Aggression, Hunting, and Human Evolution*. Berkeley: University of California Press.

25. Seligman, B. Z. 1950. "The Problem of Incest and Exogamy: A Restatement." *American Anthropologist* 52:305–16. Barnard, A. 2011. *Social*

Anthropology and Human Evolution. New York: Cambridge University Press.

26. Hrdy, S.B. 1999. *The Woman That Never Evolved.* Cambridge, MA: Harvard University Press. Hrdy, S.B. 1999. *Mother Nature: Maternal Instincts and How They Shape the Human Species.* New York: Pantheon. Hrdy, S.B. 2009. *Mothers and Others: The Evolutionary Origins of Mutual Understanding.* Cambridge, MA: Harvard University Press,.

27. Gettler, L.T. 2010. "Direct Male Care and Hominin Evolution: Why Male-Child Interaction Is More Than a Nice Social Idea." *American Anthropologist* 112:7–21. Gray, P.B., and K.G. Anderson. 2010. *Fatherhood: Evolution and Human Paternal Behavior.* Cambridge, MA: Harvard University Press. Gettler, L.T., T.W. McDade, A.B. Feranil, and C.W. Kuzawa. 2011. "Longitudinal Evidence That Fatherhood Decreases Testosterone in Human Males." *Proceedings of the National Academy of Sciences, USA,* 108:16194–99.

28. Fortes, M. 1983. *Rules and the Emergence of Society.* Occasional Paper 39, Royal Anthropological Institute of Great Britain and Ireland.

29. Coontz, S. 2005. *Marriage, a History: From Obedience to Intimacy, or How Love Conquered Marriage.* New York: Viking.

30. Eagly, A.H., and W. Wood. 1999. "The Origins of Sex Differences in Human Behavior: Evolved Dispositions versus Social Roles." *American Psychologist* 54:408–23.

31. Geary, D.C., J. Vigil, and J. Byrd-Craven. 2004. "Evolution of Human Mate Choice." *Journal of Sex Research* 41:27–42; Schmitt, D.P. 2010. "Human Mate Choice." In *Human Evolutionary Biology,* ed. M. Muehlenbein. New York: Cambridge University Press, pp. 295–308. Kirshenbaum, S. 2011. *The Science of Kissing: What Our Lips Are Telling Us.* New York: Hachette.

32. Fuentes, A. 2012. *Race, Monogamy, and Other Lies They Told You: Busting Myths about Human Nature.* Berkeley: University of California Press,.

33. Rose, H., and S. Rose, eds. 2000. *Alas Poor Darwin.* London: Jonathan Cape. Henrich. J., S.J. Heine, and A. Norenzayan. 2010. "Most People Are Not WEIRD." *Nature* 466:29. Bolhuis, J.J., G.R. Brown, R.C. Richardson, and K.N. Laland. 2011. "Darwin in Mind: New Opportunities for Evolutionary Psychology." *PLoS Biol* 9: e1001109.

34. Campbell, C.J. 2007. "Primate Sexuality and Reproduction." In *Primates in Perspective,* ed. C.J. Campbell, A. Fuentes, and K.C. MacKinnon. New York: Oxford University Press, pp. 423–37. Martin, R.D. 2013. *How We Do It: The Evolution and Future of Human Reproduction.* New York: Basic Books.

35. Berra, T.M., G. Alvarez, and F.C. Ceballos. 2010. "Was the Darwin/Wedgwood Dynasty Adversely Affected by Consanguinity?" *BioScience* 60:376–83.

36. Caspari, R., and S.-H. Lee. 2004. "Older Age Becomes Common Late in Human Evolution." *Proceedings of the National Academy of Sciences, USA,* 101:10895–900.

37. Hill, K., and A.M. Hurtado. 2012. "Social Science: Human Reproductive Assistance." *Nature* 483:160–61. And although undertheorized, it probably stands to reason that grandpa would be there too.

38. Frazer, J.G. 1900. *The Golden Bough.* Vol. 1. 2nd ed. London: Macmillan, p. 288.

39. De Waal, F. 2013. *The Bonobo and the Atheist: In Search of Humanism among the Primates.* New York: W.W. Norton.

40. Durkheim, E. 1915. *The Elementary Forms of the Religious Life.* London: George Allen and Unwin. Geertz, C. 1966. "Religion as a Cultural System." In *Anthropological Approaches to the Study of Religion,* ed. Michael P. Banton. London: Tavistock, pp. 1–46.

41. Malinowski, B. 1935. *Coral Gardens and Their Magic.* London: Allen and Unwin. Radin, P. 1937. "Economic Factors in Primitive Religion." *Science & Society* 1:310–25. King, B.J. 2007. *Evolving God: A Provocative View on the Origins of Religion.* New York: Random House.

42. Goodenough, U., and T.W. Deacon. 2003. "From Biology to Consciousness to Morality." *Zygon* 38:801–19. Deacon, T., and T. Cashman. 2009. "The Role of Symbolic Capacity in the Origins of Religion." *Journal for the Study of Religion, Nature and Culture,* 3:490–517. Wilson, D.S. 2010. *Darwin's Cathedral: Evolution, Religion, and the Nature Of Society.* Chicago: University of Chicago Press. Boehm, C. 2012. *Moral Origins: The Evolution of Virtue, Altruism, and Shame.* New York: Basic Books.

CHAPTER SEVEN. HUMAN NATURE/CULTURE

1. Powell, A., S. Shennan, and M.G. Thomas. 2009. "Late Pleistocene Demography and the Appearance of Modern Human Behavior." *Science* 324:1298–1301.

2. For the evolution of new kinship patterns, see Flannery, K., and J. Marcus. 2013. *The Creation of Inequality: How Our Prehistoric Ancestors Set the Stage for Monarchy, Slavery, and Empire.* Cambridge, MA: Harvard University Press. For the evolution of friendship, see Terrell, J. 2014. *A Talent for Friendship: Rediscovery of a Remarkable Trait.* New York: Oxford University Press.

3. Linnaeus, C. 1758. *Systema Naturae.* 10th ed. Stockholm: Laurentii salvii [Lars Salvius].

4. Ripley, W.Z. 1899. *The Races of Europe.* New York: D. Appleton. Seligman, C.G. 1930. *The Races of Africa.* Oxford: Oxford University Press. Coon, C.S. 1939. *The Races of Europe.* Cambridge, MA: Harvard University Press.

5. Huxley, J. 1931. *Africa View.* London: Chatto and Windus.

6. Brattain, M. 2007. "Race, Racism, and Antiracism: UNESCO and the Politics of Presenting Science to the Postwar Public." *American Historical Review* 112:1386–1413. Muller-Wille, S. 2007. "Race et appartenance ethnique: La diversité humaine et l'UNESCO Déclarations sur la race 1950 et 1951." In *60 Ans d'histoire de l'UNESCO, Actes du Colloque International, Paris, 16–18 Novembre 2005.* Paris: UNESCO, pp. 211–20. Selcer, P. 2012. "Beyond the Cephalic Index." *Current Anthropology* 53S5:S173-S184.

7. Weiner, J.S. 1957. "Physical Anthropology—An Appraisal." *American Scientist* 45:75–79.

8. Lewontin, R.C. 1972. "The Apportionment of Human Diversity." *Evolutionary Biology* 6:381–98. Templeton, A.R. 1998. "Human Races: A Genetic and Evolutionary Perspective." *American Anthropologist* 100:632–50. Madrigal, L., and G. Barbujani. 2007. "Partitioning of Genetic Variation in Human Populations and the Concept of Race." In *Anthropological Genetics: Theory, Methods and Applications,* ed. M.H. Crawford. New York: Cambridge University Press, pp. 19–37. Long, J.C., and R.A. Kittles. 2009. "Human Genetic Diversity and the Nonexistence of Biological Races." *Human Biology* 81:777–98.

9. Montagu, A. 1942. *Man's Most Dangerous Myth: The Fallacy of Race.* New York: Columbia University Press. Marks, J. 1995. *Human Biodiversity: Genes, Race, and History.* Piscataway, NJ: Aldine/Transaction. Tattersall, I., and R. DeSalle. 2011. *Race? Debunking a Scientific Myth.* College Station: Texas A&M University Press. Sussman, R. W. 2014. *The Myth of Race: The Troubling Persistence of an Unscientific Idea.* Cambridge, MA: Harvard University Press.

10. Krieger, N. 2005. "Embodiment: A Conceptual Glossary for Epidemiology." *Journal of Epidemiology and Community Health* 59:350–55. Duster, T. 2007. "Medicalisation of Race." *Lancet* 369:702–4. Gravlee, C. C. 2009. "How Race Becomes Biology: Embodiment of Social Inequality." *American Journal of Physical Anthropology* 139:47–57.

11. Hirszfeld, L., and H. Hirszfeld. 1919. "Serological Differences between the Blood of Different Races." *The Lancet* 2 (18 October): 675–79.

12. Snyder, L. H. 1926. "Human Blood Groups: Their Inheritance and Racial Significance." *American Journal of Physical Anthropology* 9:233–63. Boyd, W. C. 1963. "Genetics and the Human Race." *Science* 140:1057–65. Marks, J. 1996. "The Legacy of Serological Studies in American Physical Anthropology." *History and Philosophy of the Life Sciences* 18:345–62.

13. Rosenberg, N. A, J. K. Pritchard, J. L. Weber, H. M. Cann, K. K. Kidd, L. A. Zhivotovsky, and M. W. Feldman. 2002. "Genetic Structure of Human Populations." *Science* 298:2181–85. Bolnick, D. A. 2008. "Individual Ancestry Inference and the Reification of Race as a Biological Phenomenon." In *Revisiting Race in a Genomic Age,* ed. B. A. Koenig, S. S.-J. Lee, and S. Richardson. Piscataway, NJ: Rutgers University Press, pp. 70–85.

14. Proctor, R. N. 2003. "Three Roots of Human Recency: Molecular Anthropology, the Refigured Acheulean, and the UNESCO Response to Auschwitz." *Current Anthropology* 44:213–39.

15. Wolpoff, M., and R. Caspari. 2000. "The Many Species of Humanity." *Anthropological Review* 63:1–17.

16. Some of the material in this section is derived from my essay "My Ancestors, Myself," which appeared in *Aeon Magazine,* http://aeon.co/magazine/being-human/jonathan-marks-neanderthal-genomics/.

17. Gruber, J.W. 1948. "The Neanderthal Controversy: 19th-century Version." *Scientific Monthly* 67:436–39. Sommer, M. 2008. "The Neandertals." In *Icons of Evolution*, ed. Brian Regal. Westport, CT: Greenwood, pp. 139–66.

18. In the words of a leading British biologist, writing ostensibly about prehistory, "When a small band of immigrants, intent upon exploiting the mineral wealth, forces its way into a barbarous country, and, in virtue of its superiority of weapons or of skill and knowledge, is able to dominate the local people, and compel it to work for them, the stamp of the alien civilization, its practises, its customs and beliefs, can be imprinted upon a large servile population." Smith, Grafton Elliot. 1917. "The Origin of the Pre-Columbian Civilization of America." *Science* 45:246.

19. Lubbock. J. 1865. *Pre-historic Times*. London: Williams and Norgate.

20. Davenport, C.B. 1928. "Race Crossing in Jamaica." *Scientific Monthly* 27:225–38. Provine, W.B. 1973. "Geneticists and the Biology of Race Crossing." *Science* 182:790–96.

21. Gates, R.R. 1947. "Specific and Racial Characters in Human Evolution." *American Journal of Physical Anthropology* 5:221–24. Coon, C.S. 1962. *The Origin of Races*. New York: Knopf. Jackson, J.P., Jr. 2005. *Science for Segregation*. New York: NYU Press.

22. Moser, S. 1992. "The Visual Language of Archaeology: A Case Study of the Neanderthals." *Antiquity* 66:831–44. Solecki, R.S. 1971. *Shanidar: The First Flower Children*. New York: Knopf. Defleur, A., T. White, P. Valensi, L. Slimak, and E. Crégut-Bonnoure. 1999. "Neanderthal Cannibalism at Moula-Guercy, Ardèche, France." *Science* 286:128–31.

23. Church, G., and E. Regis. 2012. *Regenesis: How Synthetic Biology Will Reinvent Nature and Ourselves*. New York: Basic Books, p. 148. http://www.spiegel.de/international/zeitgeist/george-church-explains-how-dna-will-be-construction-material-of-the-future-a-877634.html. http://www.dailymail.co.uk/news/article-2265402/Adventurous-human-woman-wanted-birth-Neanderthal-man-Harvard-professor.html.

24. Cann, R.L., M. Stoneking, and A.C. Wilson. 1987. "Mitochondrial DNA and Human Evolution." *Nature* 325:31–36. Pääbo, S. 2014. *Neanderthal Man: In Search of Lost Genomes*. New York: Basic Books.

25. Mueller, F.M. 1888. *Biographies of Words and the Home of the Aryas.* London: Longmans, Green, p. 120.

26. Villa, P., and W. Roebroeks. 2014. "Neandertal Demise: An Archaeological Analysis of the Modern Human Superiority Complex." *PLoS ONE* 94: e96424. doi:10.1371/journal.pone.0096424

27. Tocheri, M.W., C.M. Orr, S.G. Larson, T. Sutikna, E.W. Saptomo, R.A. Due, T. Djubiantono, M.J. Morwood, and W.L. Jungers. 2007. "The Primitive Wrist of *Homo floresiensis* and Its Implications for Hominin Evolution." *Science* 317:1743–45. Gordon, A.D., L. Nevell, and B. Wood. 2008. "The *Homo floresiensis* Cranium LB1.: Size, Scaling, and Early Homo Affinities." *Proceedings of the National Academy of Sciences* 105:4650–55. Jungers, W., W. Harcourt-Smith, R. Wunderlich, M. Tocheri, S. Larson, T. Sutikna, R.A. Due, and M. Morwood. 2009. "The Foot of *Homo floresiensis.*" *Nature* 459:81–84. Morwood, M.J., and W.L. Jungers. 2009. "Conclusions: Implications of the Liang Bua Excavations for Hominin Evolution and Biogeography." *Journal of Human Evolution* 57:640–48. Eckhardt, R.B., M. Henneberg, A.S. Weller, and K.J. Hsü. 2014. "Rare Events in Earth History Include the LB1 Human Skeleton from Flores, Indonesia, as a Developmental Singularity, Not a Unique Taxon." *Proceedings of the National Academy of Sciences* 111:11961–966.

28. Reich, D., R.E. Green, M. Kircher, J. Krause, N. Patterson, E.Y. Durand, B. Viola, A.W. Briggs, U. Stenzel, P.L.F. Johnson, et al. 2010. "Genetic History of an Archaic Hominin Group from Denisova Cave in Siberia." *Nature* 468:1053–60. The distinguished primate anatomist and wag Bob Martin calls them "Fingabonians."

29. Reich, D., N. Patterson, M. Kircher, F. Delfin, M.R. Nandineni, I. Pugach, A.M.-S. Ko, Y.-C. Ko, T.A. Jinam, M.E. Phipps, et al. 2013. "Denisova Admixture and the First Modern Human Dispersals into Southeast Asia and Oceania." *American Journal of Human Genetics* 89:516–28.

30. Prüfer, K., F. Racimo, N. Patterson, F. Jay, S. Sankararaman, S. Sawyer, A. Heinze, G. Renaud, P.H. Sudmant, C. de Filippo, et al. 2014. "The Complete Genome Sequence of a Neanderthal from the Altai Mountains." *Nature* 505:43–49.

31. Meyer, M., Q. Fu, A. Aximu-Petri, I. Glocke, B. Nickel, J.-L. Arsuaga, I. Martínez, A. Gracia, J.M.B. de Castro, and E. Carbonell.

2013. "A Mitochondrial Genome Sequence of a Hominin from Sima de los Huesos." *Nature* 505:403–6.

32. Huerta-Sánchez, E., X. Jin, Z. Bianba, B. M. Peter, N. Vinckenbosch, Y. Liang, X. Yi, M. He, M. Somel, and P. Ni. 2014. "Altitude Adaptation in Tibetans Caused by Introgression of Denisovan-Like DNA." *Nature* 512:194–97.

33. Cavalli-Sforza, L. L., A. Piazza, P. Menozzi, and J. Mountain. 1988. "Reconstruction of Human Evolution: Bringing Together Genetic, Archaeological, and Linguistic Data." *Proceedings of the National Academy of Sciences, USA*, 85:6002–6.

34. Sneath, P. H. A. 1975. "Cladistic Representation of Reticulate Evolution." *Systematic Zoology* 243:360–68. Legendre, P. 2000. "Reticulate Evolution: From Bacteria to Philosopher." *Classification* 17:153–57. Arnold, M. 2009. *Reticulate Evolution and Humans: Origins and Ecology.* New York: Oxford University Press.

35. Shoumatoff, A. 1985. *The Mountain of Names.* New York: Simon & Schuster. Cann, R. L. 1988. "DNA and Human Origins." *Annual Review of Anthropology* 17:127–43.

36. Ralph, P., and G. Coop. 2013. "The Geography of Recent Genetic Ancestry across Europe." *PLoS Biol* 11: e1001555.

37. Rohde, D. L. T., S. Olson, and J. T. Chang. 2004. "Modelling the Recent Common Ancestry of All Living Humans." *Nature* 431:562–66.

38. For example, by ancient polymorphisms resulting from balancing selection, or heterozygote advantage. Gokcumen, O., Q. Zhu, L. C. Mulder, R. C. Iskow, C. Austermann, C. D. Scharer, T. Raj, J. M. Boss, S. Sunyaev, and A. Price. 2013. "Balancing Selection on a Regulatory Region Exhibiting Ancient Variation That Predates Human–Neandertal Divergence." *PLoS Genetics* 94: e1003404.

39. Holtzman, N. 1999. "Are Genetic Tests Adequately Regulated?" *Science* 286:409.

40. Bryan, W. J. 1922. "God and Evolution." *New York Times*, 26 February.

41. Dawkins, R. 1976. *The Selfish Gene.* New York: Oxford University Press. Buss, D. 1994. *The Evolution of Desire.* New York: Basic Books. Wrangham, R., and D. Peterson. 1996. *Demonic Males: Apes and the Origins of Human Violence.* Boston: Houghton Mifflin. Thornhill, R., and

C. T. Palmer. 2001. *A Natural History of Rape: Biological Bases of Sexual Coercion.* Cambridge, MA: MIT Press. Wade, N. 2014. *A Troublesome Inheritance: Genes, Race and Human History.* New York: Penguin.

42. For a particularly egregious example, see Cochran, G., and H. Harpending. 2009. *The 10,000 Year Explosion: How Civilization Accelerated Human Evolution.* New York: Basic Books.

43. Ingram, C.J.E., C.A. Mulcare, Y. Itan, M.G. Thomas, and D.M. Swallow. 2009. "Lactose Digestion and the Evolutionary Genetics of Lactase Persistence." *Human Genetics* 124:579–91. Curry, A. 2013. "The Milk Revolution." *Nature* 500:20–22.

44. Richardson, S.S. 2011. "Race and IQ in the Postgenomic Age: The Microcephaly Case." *BioSocieties* 6:420–46.

45. Dobzhansky, T., and M. Montagu. 1947. "Natural Selection and the Mental Capacities of Mankind." *Science* 105:587–90. Lasker, G. 1969. "Human Biological Adaptability." *Science* 166:1480–86. Gluckman, P.D., M.A. Hanson, and H.G. Spencer. 2005. "Predictive Adaptive Responses and Human Evolution." *Trends in Ecology and Evolution* 20:527–33. Kuzawa, C.W., and J.M. Bragg. 2012. "Plasticity in Human Life History Strategy: Implications for Contemporary Human Variation and the Evolution of Genus *Homo*." *Current Anthropology* 53:S369-S382.

46. Potts, R. 1996. *Humanity's Descent.* New York: William Morrow.

47. Lahr, M.M., and R.A. Foley. 1998. "Towards a Theory of Modern Human Origins: Geography, Demography, and Diversity in Recent Human Evolution." *Yearbook of Physical Anthropology* 41:137–76. Goldstein, D.B., and L. Chikhi. 2002. "Human Migrations and Population Structure: What We Know and Why It Matters." *Annual Review of Genomics and Human Genetics* 3:129–52.

INDEX